The Cost of Poor Culture

The massive financial opportunity in an enhanced workplace climate

By
Nick A. Shepherd

EduVision Inc.

D1257372

The Cost of Poor Culture

ISBN 978-1-7775703-4-7

Cover design by: EduVision Inc.
Edited by Frances Watkins

By the same author
Variance Analysis for Cost Performance Measurement
Governance, Accountability and Sustainable Development: An agenda for the 21st Century
The Controllers Handbook (2nd edition)
Reflective Leaders and High-Performance Organizations (jointly with Dr. Peter Smyth)
How Accountants Lost Their Balance
Corporate Culture – Combining Purpose and Values

Dedication

To future generations – that we find ways to improve and enhance our economic systems so that their social impact benefits all stakeholders and no longer is biased towards providers of capital.

To all those I have known in my lifetime in the many organizations and countries that I have had the opportunity to work, which has allowed me to personally develop an appreciation for human uniqueness and differences.

To Dr. Peter Smyth of The Counselling Institute, whose fellowship, insights, and support have taught me so much about understanding and valuing the human personality, and to Dr. Stewart Desson, founder, and CEO of Lumina Learning, UK, for the work that he and his team have done to advance and share our understanding of human behavior.

To my family, especially my wife Janet, for a wonderful life of love and learning.

The Cost of Poor Culture

Contents

The Cost of Poor Culture

Foreword

What is the cost of poor culture? Poor culture results in a combination of lost opportunities through operational and financial surprises, invisible excess costs, and several areas of lost opportunity.

As business has shifted towards a more human-centric approach, where knowledge and intellectual capability bring competitive advantage, culture has become increasingly important. Sadly, traditional approaches to governance, including risk management, internal controls, and financial reporting, provide little help in identifying the impact of culture on an organization's performance. Because of this, the actions often needed to bring about a more positive culture are not seen as creating a return on investment.

Corporate culture may have become a new buzzword, but it is a critical strategic success factor. It may be arrogant to try and make a judgement on whether a culture is good or bad, and this book does not attempt to do so. However, it will help the reader to look for the signs that a culture is great, good, average, or poor.

What is culture? It is "the way things are done" and is unique to each organization based on the type of business, its history, ownership, location, regulations, leadership, and other factors. An organization represents a system that has brought together different resources with the goal of developing and delivering products or services.

Each stakeholder, often defined as "anyone who is impacted by, or has an impact on the organization," provides different resources and has different needs. An organization that is able to bring these different resources together most effectively creates a competitive advantage; this usually brings benefits to all stakeholders, together with enhanced performance and reduced risk.

The more engaged and satisfied stakeholders are, the greater will be the benefits to everyone – thus an organization's culture might vary as changing events result in change and disruption. The greater the cultural strength, the more resilient the organization will be to such change, and the more resilient it is to change, the greater the probability of survival and sustainability.

Nick Shepherd
Ottawa, March 2021

1 Executive summary

Many years ago, Dr. Joseph Juran, a pioneer in quality management, referred to the "cost of quality" as the "hidden gold in the mine." Organizations that heeded his advice and started to investigate the costs of poor quality, soon realized that there was much more to effective quality management than meeting specifications and keeping customers happy. It was about saving money and improving profits.

Today the focus has shifted to the critical importance of human resources as a competitive advantage. Yet, for many organizations, their HR focus is failing to deliver the opportunities that exist. There is, once again, "gold in the mine" – but now, it is the hidden costs of poor culture. While leaders focus on developing human resource (HR) metrics, few organizations link this focus on people and relationships, with the financial impacts and benefits that would result.

The costs of poor culture exist in three aspects of organizational performance, most of which are invisible. First, there are the financial surprises. These can be fines, penalties and losses that occur when unplanned or unexpected behavior creates an unexpected financial impact. Financial surprises are the unseen risk of poor culture.

Next are the hidden costs. Buried within existing financial expenses can be major costs reflecting disengaged employees and dysfunctional relationships: the impact of poor leadership and relationships internally; a lack of understanding of corporate purpose; a failure to understand behavioral expectations around collaboration, and cooperation; poor communications; external relationships built on win / lose rather than mutually sought benefits and improvements; and actions by employees that harm the brand, reputation, and loyalty. Many of these are buried in annual operating costs. What do these amount to? How much benefit could an improved culture deliver to bottom line performance?

Then there are the lost opportunities: suggested improvements by employees that have been ignored, or the failure to base customer or supplier relationships on mutual long-term benefit. There is no magic in continuous improvement, which can only come from an engaged, interested, and committed workforce.

Yet the benefits go way beyond surprises, hidden costs, and lost opportunities. Many organizations are spending massive amounts of money, investing in intangibles, including the workforce. These costs are seen as an investment in the future. Yet traditional financial reporting not only fails to identify these investments, but it also fails to recognize them as assets that are contributing to the value of the business. While the human resources sector is developing metrics for integrated reporting, the financial impact of effective HR management – underpinned by a positive culture – remains hidden.

This book is based on the author's knowledge and involvement in the cost of poor quality, both from spending some time as Chair of the Quality Costs Committee of the American Society of Quality, and as a workshop facilitator and consultant. This experience has been used to develop a similar framework for understanding the costs of poor culture (COPC); while the approach is not an exact science, it defines a framework and thinking process for identifying the hidden costs and follows this with a suggested implementation plan. The book also provides links to the developing ISO standards on human resource management, in particular the guidelines and technical specifications on HR metrics. It also links with the concept of integrated reporting.

To provide a context for the importance of organizational culture, the early chapters describe the evolution from a tangibles-based business model to one where intangibles are the prime drivers of value creation. This information can also provide a bridge to the author's book *Corporate Culture – Combining Purpose and Values*.

As we enter a new world, in which organizations must transition to become increasingly people-centric, this book illustrates that corporate culture is a critical success factor for corporate strategy, which must start at the highest levels and permeate every aspect of an organization's behavior. The benefits are not just to be a better corporate citizen, but to build an enhanced, higher performing, and sustainable enterprise.

2 What is the problem?

The impact of having an unplanned or poor culture has rather crept up on society; now that certain aspects are being realized, there is a chorus of ideas about how to fix it that range from getting rid of capitalism and replacing it with something else to new governance approaches, new legislation, new reporting systems among many other remedies. What has been happening?

Value	Human capital has become a key creator of organizational value
Behavior	Human behavior has become as important as organizational purpose
Cost	Spending on people is opaque, misunderstood and poorly reported
Reporting	Annual reports and audits provide little assurance of organizational risk outside financial aspects

2.1 The underlying changes

Value. With the evolution of the fourth industrial revolution – the knowledge economy or whatever name one wants to apply – people, the use of intellectual capital, technology and relationships have become the drivers of value creation. Almost all drivers of improved organizational performance – output, cost, revenue, and quality – come from initiatives in innovation and creativity, which, in turn, are the product of collaboration, cooperation, communication, and commitment. This has brought with it a shift in how people need to be managed. No longer is motivation and commitment (or engagement) important, it is now strategically critical. Competitive advantage is no longer in having the smartest people but in creating the most positive work atmosphere.

Behavior. It is evident that people's behavior is important; many organizations have incurred financial penalties for employees who break the law or act unethically. Such poor behavior extends from the lowest to the highest levels. Many organizations have implemented codes of conduct or codes of ethics; regulators have strengthened the responsibilities of senior executives for ensuring that effective controls are in place, requiring certifications such as those demanded under SOX.

Poor behavior often comes from people thinking they are doing "the right thing." This has created more challenges for managers: there is usually no legal remedy for many actions that society might see as unethical but which the organization may see as a competitive advantage (or even a necessity when others are also doing it). This behavioral problem has been made worse by outsourcing and globalization – where legal and ethical standards can be significantly different between certain countries. This risk of human behavior in the supply chain also has an impact on the reputation of the buying organization.

Cost. While labor costs remain one of the most significant expenditures for organizations, "where the money goes" has changed considerably. Historically, the greatest labor cost was for people engaged in the creation and delivery of the products or services that generate current revenues. Today, a large portion of labor cost is for carrying out activities that have a longer-term benefit to the organization. Examples would include building and maintaining customer relationships; building and maintaining supply chains; working with customers and suppliers to develop new products and services; and generating new and innovative ways to change current activities and processes to reduce costs for the future. In effect, these costs are spent to build value for the future but because of accounting standards they are almost all treated as current expenses and written off against current income. This has created all sorts of problems in organizational valuation, the greatest being that they do not show up in the accounting records as having any value. (This is because accounting considers them intangibles which cannot be shown as an asset.)

As an example, if an organization now spends twice the amount it used to spend per person on recruitment so as to improve their quality of hire and reduce turnover, there is no reported financial benefit of these changes; in fact, the higher HR costs are charged against current earnings (even though they bring future benefits) and thus they appear to reduce profitability. The same is true of training and development costs. By spending to invest in its work force, an organization is building value for the future, yet if this value becomes impaired, the impact is not visible. (In fact, it may be hidden if short-term actions are taken to improve short-term profitability, such as cutting off all training.)

Reporting. Historically, corporate reporting and accountability has focused on financial disclosures; this was valid because, historically, many organizations were financially capital intensive.

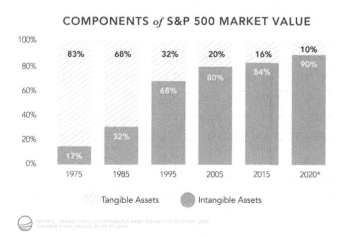

COMPONENTS *of* S&P 500 MARKET VALUE

The Ocean Tomo[1] chart shows how this has changed: in 1975, 83% of the value of the S&P 500 companies was represented by what is called "book value," i.e., the value according to accounting standards. As the world has been changing and the approach to expenditure on intangibles has not, this accounting value has declined to a situation where only about 10% of an investor's value is represented by accounting records. This is because much more money is being spent on things that are invisible.

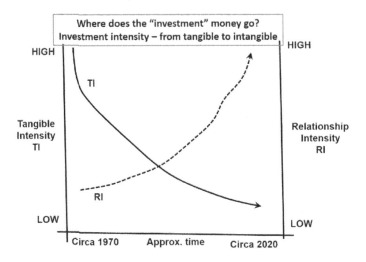

The graph shows that, over the same period as the value change above, tangible intensity (TI) has declined, and relationship intensity (RI) has grown. Yet all the money spent on developing this value has been invisible. As discussed, in a human-centric world, much of value creation develops because of internal and external relationship building.

This change has also meant that a significantly higher portion of organizational risk comes from intangibles: loss of people; loss of brand value or reputation; and loss of supply chain capability. Yet almost none of these risks are evident from most annual reports. For example, for

---

[1] Used with permission, Ocean Tomo Intangible Asset Market Value Study

many years, non-financial organizations have been publishing and commenting on the brand values of key organizations.

Jan 1st 2020	Market Value	Brand Value	Book Value	Other Intangibles	Brand Value	Book Value	Other Intangibles
Facebook	$647,840	$79,804	$105,306	$462,730	12.3%	16.3%	71.4%
Apple	$1,581,000	$234,241	$78,423	$1,268,336	14.8%	5.0%	80.2%
Amazon	$1,376,000	$220,791	$65,368	$1,089,841	16.0%	4.8%	79.2%
Netflix	$200,680	$22,945	$9,334	$168,401	11.4%	4.7%	83.9%
Google (+)	$967,990	$167,713	$203,659	$596,618	17.3%	21.0%	61.6%
	$4,773,510	$725,494	$462,089	$3,585,927	15.2%	9.7%	75.1%

This chart[2] shows the significance of brand value: at the beginning of 2020, investors (the market) valued Amazon at $1.4 trillion, yet its accounts (book value) reported $65.3 billion of financial assets and its brand value was reported to be about $220.8 billion. This means that almost $1.1. trillion of its market value was represented by "other intangibles," in other words, those things that Amazon had spent money developing but which were not included as financial assets. By 2021 these numbers had significantly *increased*.

While using market prices as a base can be seen as dubious, it remains important that the value of over $1 trillion was coming from something that was invisible. It was "the value of the system" that had been created to earn income. If this system had been impaired, almost nothing in reporting would tell the story; nor would a financial audit because these intangibles are outside the scope of audit reporting. Other than profit, there is no system-wide indicator that tells us the health of the all the component aspects.

2.2   Alternative and integrated reporting

There have been several milestones in the journey towards enhanced reporting. The desire for information about the human aspect of

---

[2] Data extracted from "Y Charts"

organizational activity remains at an early stage – although the first annual report of Ben and Jerry's Ice Cream, which addressed the **Triple Bottom Line** of people, planet, and profits, was in produced in 1987. The journey of change so far has been marked by several stages. **Total Quality Management** (also known at TQM) in the 1970s and 1980s brought about a realization that if people were left out of the efforts to improve product or service quality, little improvement would be achieved.

There was also a growing realization that employee behavior was important, leading to legislation such as the **US Foreign Corrupt Practices Act** of 1977. The issue of employee behavior has remained a theme since then, with organizations developing codes of conduct, codes of ethics and ethical practices, and other guidance to frame the expected behaviors. In reality, employee behavior is an ongoing challenge and one strategy to address it is the focus on corporate culture.

As the strategy of outsourcing grew, it quickly became apparent that many organizations and countries within which the outsourced facilities operated had poor labor standards. Safety issues, fires, equipment failures, child employment, strong autocratic leadership, together with laws and practices that forbid employees to organize, all contributed to scandals. As corporate social responsibility grew, starting with a certification standard on social accountability (SA 8000) in 1989, progressive suppliers could demonstrate that they were developing, maintaining, and applying socially acceptable practices in the workplace. This development of "good practices" has continued and now includes the International Standard, ISO 26000 *Guidance on Social Responsibility*.

During this period, various voluntary frameworks had been developing for "non-financial" reporting. The challenge was that several countries had different statutory requirements and other groups such as investors were also beginning to ask for additional information. Shareholders were concerned about environmental issues and started requiring information as part of the **Carbon Disclosure Program (CDP)**. Regulators were looking for guidance in the USA and the Sustainability Accounting Standards Board (SASB) was created in 2011 to issue guidelines. Countries and regulators started to become increasingly concerned around the variety of information and the lack of consistency; this was one key space that the framework developers, such as the **Global Reporting Initiative (GRI)** moved in to, creating a great foundation of recommended approaches.

The reporting challenge had also become more complex because organizations were faced with different statutory demands for reporting financial information, environmental issues and matters of health and safety. There was also an evolving framework of "leading practices," such as GRI. Overlaying all of this was the social feedback that organizations were tracking, through which society was looking for other areas related to corporate accountability. One can depict it this way:

Reporting area	Statutory	Leading practices	Optional
Financial	Global and / or national standards	Limited	Limited
Environmental	Some – national	Yes – e.g., GRI	Yes
Health & Safety	Some – national	Yes	Yes
Social (community / philanthropy, ethical)	Limited	Yes – e.g., GRI	Yes

While financial reporting had some 100 years of maturity behind it and was also well supported by both legislated requirements and globally or nationally accepted standards, most other reporting was a patchwork of nationally developed approaches, plus developing frameworks for leading practices, supplemented by what each organization felt was important to its own investors and owners, and its reputation and credibility.

By 2012, it was becoming apparent that the traditional financial reports and these emerging supplemental reports, which now addressed several issues including aspects of "people," needed to be brought together. An international committee was formed, the **International Integrated Reporting Committee (IIRC)** to research, consult, develop and propose a new framework for corporate reporting. The IIRC issued its first framework in 2013, which was followed by several years of experimentation, with an updated set of guidelines in early 2021.

Finally, in 2015, the United Nations (UN) issued its **Sustainable Development Goals (SDGs)**, also known as the Global Goals, which were adopted by all UN Member States. This was a universal call to action to end poverty, protect the planet and ensure that all people enjoy peace and prosperity by 2030. While these goals did not have mandatory reporting status, they did begin to influence social policy on a national basis. Given the importance of the corporate sector in many of the UN SDGs, these also began to influence corporate reporting as well as national policy and legislation.

By 2020, this evolution in demand for enhanced reporting reached a point of consolidation and focus. The following statement was released in late 2020[3]:

> "The five framework- and standard-setting institutions of international significance, CDP, the Climate Disclosure Standards Board (CDSB), the Global Reporting Initiative (GRI), the International Integrated Reporting Council (IIRC) and the Sustainability Accounting Standards Board (SASB), have co-published a shared vision of the elements necessary for more comprehensive corporate reporting and a joint statement of intent to drive towards this goal – by working together and by each committing to engage with key actors, including IOSCO and the IFRS, the European Commission, and the World Economic Forum's International Business Council.

---

[3] Press release 11th September 2020 by participating bodies

In 2013 when the IIRC issued its original guidelines, there was a hope that these would be universally adopted by 2020 but this did not happen. However, the cost and complexity of reporting did bring together many of the key players to collaborate on moving forward as seen in the press release.

The International Federation of Accountants (IFAC) also issued a joint press release[4] with the IIRC in early 2021, indicating their agreement to work together to develop approaches for "assurance" of integrated reports moving forward – a role that accountants have held globally for financial reporting for many, many years.

> "To help meet this demand (for added assurance), and to increase confidence in integrated reporting, the International Federation of Accountants (IFAC) and the International Integrated Reporting Council (IIRC) today, 26 February 2021, are launching a new joint initiative, Accelerating Integrated Reporting Assurance in the Public Interest

Finally, if this was not enough indication of impending change in reporting, the UK Government (Department for Business, Energy and Industrial Strategy) issued a consultative paper on changing the approach to audits[5]:

> "Audit to extend beyond financial results, looking at wider performance and ESG [environmental, social and governance] targets."

Change is coming. In early 2021 the IIRC and SASB announced that they were merging.

---

[4] Wording of press release as reported by ICAS March 3rd, 2021
[5] "Restoring trust in audit and corporate governance: proposals on reforms"

3 Where are the costs of poor culture hiding?

The evolution in business and the changing importance of human behaviors might – or probably should – raise fear in the hearts of accountants, investors, and boards of directors: There are all sorts of different and possibly irrational people out there, who all think differently and are making day-to-day decisions in their organizations – especially since these behavioral aspects apply equally to senior managers and "C-suite" executives! No wonder that culture is becoming recognized as something that is important in organizational performance. The important question though is: Does it really matter?

There are three key risks that impact financial performance related to poor culture (or lower level of maturity) – the problem is that in almost all situations, current financial reporting does a poor job of highlighting such risks, and when they are reflected, it often occurs after the event. These risks are:

- **Financial surprises** Unanticipated impacts on financial performance that occur due to control failures and unanticipated behavior (examples would be legal and regulatory fines and penalties, as well as negative impacts in areas such as brand and reputation).
- **Buried costs** The impacts of lower or poor financial performance that come from restraints on value creation, that result in lower output, higher costs, lower revenues and lower quality of products and services.

- **Lost opportunities** to enhance value, which come from opportunities to increase output, lower costs, increase revenues and enhance quality.

Financial surprises are typically unanticipated, have a negative impact on earnings, and will usually reduce organizational value. In the second situation, buried impacts caused by "sub-optimization" are often not visible, as the higher operating costs are buried within the existing expenses. While performance benchmarking might indicate an opportunity for improvement, the excess costs are not clearly reported or understood – it's just "what it is." Often, as a result of these perceived excess costs, organizations resort to short-term cost-cutting measures like layoffs, which might have short-term benefits but, in the longer term, do little to enhance cultural maturity; such measures deplete intangible value, often causing deterioration in employee morale and other areas such as client and supplier relationships. These then further reduce morale and motivation to create a "vicious circle."

The third area of lost opportunity is the most strategically critical. Most organizations develop performance improvement budgets but rarely is the question asked, - how much better could performance be if everything and everyone was operating as a fully effective, aligned, and holistic system?

It is interesting that when the **Cost of Poor Quality (COPQ)** was developed as an approach to understanding the impact of poor quality on financial performance, a definition was developed[6] and is still used today. This provides the basis for understanding the question above as it applied at the time to the goal of increased quality and reads as follows:

---

[6] From: *Principles of Quality Costs* (1999), *3rd* edition. Jack Campanella and ASQ Quality Costs Committee, Quality Press.

> **Definition**
>
> **Total quality costs** represent the difference between the actual cost of a product or service and what the reduced cost would be if there were no possibility of sub-standard service, failure of products, or defects in their manufacture.

Whole-system proponents have been exploring optimum performance for years; the **Theory of Constraints (TOC)** was one such approach that demonstrated the potential improvements available from those who had moved to a more "systems thinking" framework[7]:

On time delivery	⬆	**60%**
Revenues increases	⬆	68%
Profit increases	⬆	82%
Inventory reduction	⬇	50%
Cycle time reduction	⬇	66%

This holistic or whole-system thinking is core to corporate culture and organizational maturity and, as will be demonstrated, can significantly reduce **organizational risk**, and enhance **operating performance**. These two factors combined enhance organizational competitiveness, increase competitive advantage, and reduce risk (thus enhancing sustainability).

3.1 Financial surprises

This category involves actions that take place that were unexpected and will typically have a negative financial impact on the organization. First some boundaries: this segment will not discuss private, owner-operated

---

[7] Quick guide to Theory of Constraints http://www.tocinstitute.org/theory-of-constraints.html

organizations, or those that may have a large portion of private ownership even if they are publicly listed. In such cases, the behavior will typically be the result of the values of the person running the organization. If that person is prepared to act illegally or unethically, then they will make that decision and there will only be the regulatory or legal system to stop them.

Examples might include scandals such as that concerning Bernie Madoff (2008), The Satyam Scandal, involving founder Ramalinga Raju (2009), Waste Management, involving founder Dean L. Buntrock (1998), and the Livent founder, Garth Drabinsky (between about 2001 and 2013). The poor, unsuspecting external investors might have had difficulty influencing the actions, penalties, and collapses in these cases.

The broader issue is where these events and surprises occur in widely held, publicly traded organizations, in which the system of governance should protect against illegal or unethical actions. One might assume, in these cases, that the events came as a surprise to those responsible. They may have occurred with board knowledge of the risk, or by management acting on its own authority or by individuals or small groups acting alone.

Financial surprises can be looked at in two groups – those caused by individual action, and those caused by the organization as a whole. Individual actions leading to surprises would include those of Nick Leeson at Barings Bank in 1995, which resulted in the bank's collapse.

This was a classic case where inattention to culture increased the risk of financial problems; if people are left to their own "devices" with little or no guidance (and poor oversight / governance) then results will be unpredictable! There is a great quote on the University of Essex website that provides a history of scandals and frauds[8] :

---

[8] https://projects.exeter.ac.uk/RDavies/arian/scandals/classic.html

> "Bankers who hire money hungry geniuses should not always express surprise and amazement when some of them turn around with brilliant, creative, and illegal means of making money."
>
> *The quotation is from a speech by the financial thriller writer Linda Davies, on "The Psychology of Risk, Speculation and Fraud", at a conference on EMU in Amsterdam.*

It appears that, even before he arrived in Singapore, the risk existed; Nick Leeson was "less than honest[9]" when applying for his broker's license. There have been several other cases of rogue traders acting alone in the financial services industry. These might be considered "control" surprises, but what about the larger corporate surprises?

Publicly available data reveal that, in the USA, penalties and fines imposed on organizations over the last 20 years have exceeded $490 billion; that is $490 billion charged for anything from safety violations to illegal acts, lack of protection of privacy, fraud, and many others.

It would be unfair to generalize about these unplanned charges – in fact, some may be the result of management decisions to accept certain levels of risk, so that when an unplanned incident occurs, paying the fine is part of the cost of doing business. The table below lists the top six in total penalties imposed:

---

[9] Scott, Hal S., 2006. *International Finance: Transactions, Policy, and Regulation.* Foundation Press.

Parent organization	Cumulative cost in $ billions
Bank of America	$82.764
JPMorgan Chase	$35.819
BP	$29.197
Citigroup	$25.454
Volkswagen	$23.780
Wells Fargo	$21.359

Probably one of the most obvious costs relative to poor culture is demonstrated by the financial meltdown between 2008 and 2010, which caused the near collapse of the financial services industry; it can be seen from the table above that banks and other financial services organizations suffered heavily from fines imposed in the years following these problems. But this was not the only problem.

Wells Fargo arrived at a $3 billion settlement in 2020[10] for offences that apparently occurred between 2002 and 2016 related to the opening of fraudulent accounts. This was a widely publicized event and had a significant impact on both the firm's reputation, value and, of course, finances!

This last example may well have been a situation caused by people doing what they thought to be acceptable. They were, after all opening these accounts based on "direction" imposed by quotas and managed by those in leadership positions. Was such illegal and unethical conduct acceptable to meet quotas?

Another example on the list is Volkswagen; many will remember this scandal, often referred to as Dieselgate, in which fuel consumption / mileage claims were generated incorrectly. Could it be that, in this situation, the engineers working in the company thought they were doing

---

[10] See NY Times and other reports

the right thing and finding a way to meet the fuel consumption require-ments? Did senior leadership even know about it? Why didn't anybody blow the whistle? What type of culture allowed this to be done?

While one can concentrate on the large number that hits the headlines, this does not tell the whole story. The top six organizations in the list account for almost 40% of the total $490 billion, yet using the data available from Violation Tracker[11], it can also be seen that there were over 480,000 individual fines and violations.

Parent organization	Cumulative cost in $ billions	# of items	Average fine or penalty
Bank of America	$82.764	219	$377.9M
Volkswagen	$23.780	57	$424.6M
Wells Fargo	$21.359	182	$117.4M
Canadian National Railways (CNR)	$0.014	559	$25,856
Union Pacific	$0.183	3,298	$55,486

For Volkswagen, three of the offences (related to Dieselgate) account for over 90% of their total fines and penalties; could this suggest that the overall governance is good but that the fuel economy lapse was more of a one-off problem? In the cases of Wells Fargo and Bank of America, the average fines are extremely high, and the number of offences is almost the same, but the average cost is lower. Does this suggest that Wells Fargo is relatively better than Bank of America?

Looking at a totally different industry, we can see that the railroads seem to have much lower average fines, although, upon investigation, it seems that almost all the events are safety-related, and the fines are much smaller. Does this tell us anything about either CNR or Union Pacific? Are these maybe the acceptable costs of doing business? However, might this contravene a safety-based culture, which is what both railroad companies

---

[11] See https://violationtracker.goodjobsfirst.org/parent-totals

The Cost of Poor Culture

are very conscious of? The fact is that ALL these events were unplanned, or if planned then clearly illegal and/or unethical. Were they sanctioned?

To these costs, particularly in financial services, can be added the prior societal impact of bailouts from various national governments; in the USA alone, the official number was about $700 billion, but broader-based assessments[12] put the numbers much higher, with $4.6 trillion paid out and a total commitment that can be up to $16.8 trillion. There would also be societal costs associated with areas such as health and safety impacts.

While it is a smaller amount, GM was fined $1 million by the Securities and Exchange Commission (SEC) over ignition switch problems that apparently killed at least 124 people (small price to pay!) on top of at least $595 million that the company paid out to victims[13]. The CEOs' responses to these fines are interesting: GM's CEO, Mary Barra, told the House Energy and Commerce Subcommittees she was aiming *"...to correct a culture that has displayed a pattern of incompetence and neglect."* This links the problem right back to behavior, but doesn't it seem to leave hanging the role of leadership? Why did people act in a way that was either unethical or illegal?

The key point in the sorts of prosecutions detailed above might be less the impact of the fines and penalties and more the damage that the conduct had on "social capital," that is, the relationships with employees and the sort of conduct they saw as acceptable. In many cases, the levels of fines amounted to a small proportion of income. (A detailed analysis was not performed because the dates of the various events, the delays and challenges of prosecution and the date the penalties were decided are almost impossible to reconcile to the income in the year or years that the events took place. Additionally, several organizations went through

---

[12] "The Big Bank Bailout," *Forbes Magazine*, July 2014 (Mike Collins). https://www.forbes.com/sites/mikecollins/2015/07/14/the-big-bank-bailout/#31bda9aa2d83

[13] *USA Today* http://www.usatoday.com/story/money/cars/2017/01/18/general-motors-securities-and-exchange-commission-sec-ignition-switch/96717570/

22

mergers and acquisitions during the period, especially in the financial services.)

As can be seen from the above examples, the costs associated with surprises can be significant, and have both financial and reputational impacts; at worst, they can lead to the collapse of a whole sector, such as the financial meltdown in 2008–2010. Financial reporting informed investors about these issues after the fact. Could investors have been better prepared for these risks? If one looks at the financial services industry, not every bank participated in the actions that led to the collapse. What was the difference? Were the other banks more prudent? Was their culture more risk averse? Did every employee understand where the line was drawn, beyond which they could not go in decision making?

If we drill down further, is it possible to say that the less risky banks' approach to hiring and compensation was more driven by hiring people with the "right values" and compensating employees and executives in a way that did not encourage undesired behavior? Was there an orientation program and was it effective? Was the whistle-blower program more effective? Was there a greater level of trust, communication, collaboration, and cooperation within the bank? How are leaders selected, developed, managed, and compensated? These are all features of the maturity and culture with which the organization is managed. If investors don't have visibility into their organization's maturity, they have little protection against surprises that reduce earnings and deplete value and, at worst, void their investment completely.

A growing category of surprises is the increase in Impairment losses that are being incurred by corporations; these happen after a merger or acquisition where the buyer pays more for the acquired organization than its book (accounting) value. In effect, the cost of buying the business as a system capable of earning an income stream is justified at this higher market price, and this "premium over book price" appears as an (intangible) asset on the buyer's financial records, recorded as "goodwill." This is obviously a cost incurred by the shareholders of the buying organization that is funded from either diluting the value of their own shares or taking on more debt. When management and/or the auditors determine that this asset (goodwill) is worth less than is shown in the records, it is considered to have been "impaired" and the amount must be taken as a financial loss. Why?

"Over the last five years, there have been a total of 1,556 events in which goodwill has been considered impaired and written off (or written down) by publicly-traded companies incorporated in the United States." The total cost of this has been $270.4 billion[14]. While there are many issues and challenges behind these numbers, a key issue is that part of what the buyer was willing to pay for was "the system" that included the culture which gave the acquisition some of its market value. Could one believe that this was a surprise?

3.2   Buried and invisible costs

Financial reporting provides limited insight into details of existing costs; for external users, costs are aggregated at an extremely high level, such as operating expenses, which might then be analyzed by cost of product and services, sales, general and administrative (SG&A), and depreciation and amortization; even internally, costs tend to be reported "by department, by type of expense." This approach often leads to reinforcing the belief that the workforce is the largest cost and, therefore, if performance is to be enhanced costs must be reduced. Interestingly, in many public financial reports, the total cost of the workforce is not published. The questions should always be: Why are the costs as high as they are? What is driving the demand for resources?

Financial reporting has been a barrier for understanding opportunities for change in the past. When quality management was being recognized as a

---

[14] https://www.duffandphelps.com/insights/publications/goodwill-impairment/2020-us-goodwill-impairment-study

key issue for business, particularly in the 1970s in North America, many CEOs couldn't see the value or benefits from investing in quality management systems. Very often the rationale was given that better quality would improve customer satisfaction; however, rarely were quality practitioners able to convince CEOs that not only would better quality save money, but the absence of it was also already costing the organization significantly higher expenses (to coin a phrase, "hidden gold in the mine.")

It was only when someone like the late Phil Crosby, in his book *Quality is Free*[15] (1979), demonstrated the benefits by dispelling the myth that improving quality would cost money and focused on the unseen opportunity, that CEOs started to come around. Crosby's "stages of maturity" in management approaches to quality demonstrate the problem, especially when metrics don't show the existing costs being incurred:

Crosby suggested there were five stages of understanding the relationship between quality and financial performance. While his estimates for the financial impact at each stage were the result of his own research, they were later validated by the level of savings identified by proponents of an approach to process improvement called Six Sigma.

The first stage of uncertainty reflected an unawareness of the hidden financial impact of poor quality; this often-reflected organizations that relied on "inspection" as their primary approach to ensuring quality. Once awareness started developing and management "awoke" to the hidden opportunities, efforts started to identify hidden costs; these costs were always there - but were never identified as being opportunities for improvement. Typically, the real "Ah Ha" moment came at level three when efforts started to build quality into the business as a "way of operating" rather than relying on inspection. It was at this point that opportunities really started to be understood and management re-allocated resources to fix the underlying causes of poor quality. As the following chapters

---

[15] Crosby, Philip, "Quality is Free," 1979, McGraw Hill

demonstrate, once resources are directed at changing the root causes of the problem, the whole "system" works more effectively and the outcomes are significantly improved.

Maturity stage	Description	Management understanding and attitude	Cost of quality as % of sales	
			Reported	Actual
1	Uncertainty	No comprehension of quality as a management tool; tend to blame quality departments for quality problems	Unknown	20.0%
2	Awakening	Recognizes that quality management may be of value but not willing to provide money or time to make it happen	3.0%	18.0%
3	Enlightenment	While going through quality improvement program learn more about quality management; becoming supportive and helpful	8.0%	12.0%
4	Wisdom	Participating; understand absolutes of quality management. Recognize their personal role in continuing emphasis	6.5%	8.0%
5	Certainty	Consider quality management an essential part of the company system.	2.5%	2.5%

At the time, many organizations were operating at Stage 1 or 2 – not realizing that buried in their costs was a possible opportunity to enhance performance by 18–20% of revenues. Almost no financial reporting was showing this, as it was buried in the existing cost of doing business; the same is true today for the cost of poor culture. The "way things are" is an embedded cost of doing business and the concept of "how much better it could be" is hard to identify and evaluate. Maybe a similar approach could be taken with the hidden costs of poor culture?

At stage one, culture might be talked about, but it is not "managed" as a "way of doing business;" it often relies upon solutions like team building and leadership training. It is only when the hidden costs of a poor culture start to be realized that culture starts to be planned and managed effectively. This involves the strategic re-allocation of resources to treating people as an investment and making them central to organizational strategy.

Culture Maturity stage	Description	Management understanding and attitude	Cost of poor culture as % of sales	
			Reported	Actual
1	Uncertainty	Culture is unplanned; surprises occur, people are the problem.	Unknown	20.0%
2	Awakening	People's behavior is unpredictable and a key risk, need for codes and training.	3.0%	18.0%
3	Enlightenment	Start to move toward people centric management.	8.0%	12.0%
4	Wisdom	Understanding of intangible trade off issues and focus on value.	6.5%	8.0%
5	Certainty	People at centre of human centric business model.	2.5%	2.5%

The values in the above table might be questionable; this will be developed and expanded later to illustrate that culture costs may be equivalent.

Buried costs form a significant part of the impact of poor culture, and many of these start with a lack of employee commitment. This not only decreases operational performance, but it also permeates almost everything that people are involved with – suppliers, customers, other employees. This results in a flawed business system that is unable to optimize performance, which often shows up in lower or inconsistent profitability. Management has two choices to fix profit – increase the income side or decrease the cost side. The challenge for management is to know where to focus to achieve the desired improvements. Profit is like the tip of an iceberg because most of what is happening is invisible.

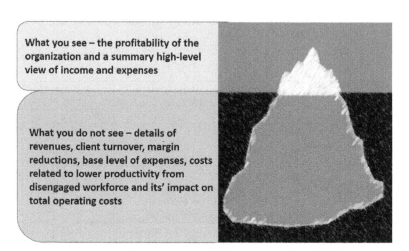

What you see – the profitability of the organization and a summary high-level view of income and expenses

What you do not see – details of revenues, client turnover, margin reductions, base level of expenses, costs related to lower productivity from disengaged workforce and its' impact on total operating costs

A poor or toxic culture results in disengaged employees who impact ALL aspects of an income statement. There has been significant research on this whole-system impact.

- Gallup estimates[16] that actively disengaged employees cost the USA between \$483 and \$605 billion each year in lost productivity.
- Overall excess turnover because of toxic workplaces has cost the US economy \$223 billion over five years[17] (by causing over 20% of employees to leave their jobs).

---

[16] "State of the American Workplace Report," 2017, Gallup.
[17] "The High Cost of a Toxic Workplace Culture," 2019, SHRM (Society of Human Resource Management).

- Poor workplaces contribute to absenteeism, and burnout costs the US economy $225.8 billion, or $1,685 per employee per year[18].
- Toxic workplaces cost the UK economy around £15.7 billion annually[19].
- *Harvard Business Review*[20] identified numerous impacts from poor culture, including 50% greater healthcare costs; 37% higher absenteeism; 18% lower productivity, and 56% lower share price over time.

An even more important observation[21] about the widespread damage that a poor culture can create is the impact of a toxic worker on the rest of the organization. The benefit from hiring a "superstar" who ranks in the top 1% of performers will generate $5,303 in savings, while *avoiding* hiring (or importantly developing) a toxic worker will generate savings of $12,489.

What are these buried costs and where are they? Some may be visible, but the majority are buried within existing operating expenses. The largest portion of such excess costs relates to employee productivity. This can cover many activities such as lower "on-the-job" productivity; spending excess time on the internet, including social media; nonproductive meetings because of poor meeting skills, including an unwillingness to cooperate and collaborate; wasted time spent looking for information that may already be available; excess absenteeism, or time off for sickness;

---

[18] CDC study published in "4 Devastating Consequences of a Toxic Workplace," Tanya Prive, November 3, 2019, Inc. https://www.inc.com/tanya-prive/4-devastating-consequences-of-a-toxic-workplace-culture.html

[19] *The Culture Economy Report 2020*, Breathe. https://www.breathehr.com/en-gb/resources/culture-economy-report-2020

[20] *Harvard Business Review*, December 1, 2015. "Proof That Positive Work Cultures Are More Productive" (Emma Seppälä and Kim Cameron). https://hbr.org/2015/12/proof-that-positive-work-cultures-are-more-productive

[21] Houseman, M., and Minor, Dylan, "Toxic Workers", Harvard Business School, Working Paper 16-057.

higher staff turnover driving higher HR costs, as well as more time spent by operational managers on hiring activity.

Given that one of the single largest costs for many organizations is money paid to employees, even a 1% improvement would result in significantly improved performance. However, the cost does not end there: studies have shown that dissatisfied employees also have a negative impact on relationships with others, such as customers, suppliers and other third parties. Again, this can reduce the productivity of these relationships.

To really understand the costs of a poor culture, the hidden excess costs need to be identified and reported and then used as a base against which a re-allocation of resources can take place. This was Crosby's and Juran's main theme - improvement would not actually cost the organization more money. What was needed was a re-allocation of resources away from the hidden expenses that were already being incurred towards investing in the underlying "root causes." However, unless there was a clear ROI from these investments' management would be reluctant to make the changes. This is why identifying the hidden costs is so important - it starts to build a foundation for a return on investment.

There is significant research available that demonstrates the benefits of "fixing" a poor culture – or as it is often referred to a toxic culture. The challenge is that many of the existing metrics do not have financial values associated with them. Using some of the examples below, it would seem obvious that turnover and absenteeism are important HR metrics and that improving these would lead to potentially improved financial performance. But how much is our current level of turnover costing the organization? What level of savings could be generated if the whole approach to hiring could be changed? Does the organization really know the root cause of turnover or absenteeism? The following table provides some examples of improvement areas and where the current impact of these events is buried or hidden; applying financial numbers to these would be revealing:

#	Benefits from enhancing Culture	Where the negative impact is hidden today
1	37% lower absenteeism	Currently buried in labour costs which translate into higher costs / unit of output; higher temporary staffing costs; customer penalties from unplanned delivery delays; quality problems from using untrained staff to fill in
2	25% lower turnover	Higher hiring and training costs; larger proportion of employees lower on the "learning curve" so output lower; excessive supervisor time spent on hiring / discipline problems
3	21% productivity improvement	Current labour costs higher relative to output; problems remain unresolved; supervisors ignore employee ideas; suggestions for improvement are unaddressed; employee ideas for machine improvements ignored; maintenance downtime higher; suppliers unwilling to share improvement ideas; higher sick leave / absenteeism; employees work in silos and fail to collaborate, communicate and share ideas
4	48% lower safety accidents and issues	Higher absenteeism for sick days (higher temp staffing / union pay adjustments / overtime costs); indirect negative impact on customers (services not provided)
5	28% lower shrinkage	Currently wastage and losses written off as higher cost of sales; can also impact time spent on inventory counts and analysis
6	41% lower defect rates	May show up as excessive scrap or rework costs but in many cases buried within existing operating costs when work is repeated to correct problems
7	10% higher customer ratings	Higher sales and support costs (e.g. call centres) to service higher levels of complaints, problems, customer turnover, returns and time spent when problems are escalated

Items 1 through 3 would reflect the lower output/productivity per person; and item 4 would suggest both excessive labor costs but also impacts on other costs, as well as, potentially, relationships with others. Item 5 typically comes as a write off, either because of poor record keeping (employees do not care about accuracy) or, worse, actual shrinkage and losses. Item 6 is a classic cost of poor quality. With all the quality processes and procedures in place, employee commitment remains a key driver of delivering on "first time right." This is an especially challenging area for the service industry as service problems may only ever show up in the load factors on call centers and other support areas. Item 7 is often a composite of improvements from other areas. However, it is well-known that "happy employees mean happy clients." The UK-based Maturity Institute[22] developed research that linked underlying operational issues to poor culture, and increased risk that can have an impact on operational effectiveness and thus costs. These might include:

Risk area	Nature of risk	Examples of operational costs impact
Systemic disconnection: reward and value outcomes	Rewards for senior executives through to management and staff do not relate to value and encourages other outcomes.	Higher absenteeism from safety issues; encourages higher turnover through poor morale which drives higher hiring costs; increase losses / theft; sales /support costs increase caused by focusing on financial returns more than client satisfaction (legal bias vs. relationship); higher overtime costs
Knowledge and learning failures	Failure to use internal knowledge; Inability to learn from mistakes	Higher process costs due to defects and repeated errors; less process improvement; problems hidden and not resolved; higher call centre costs (repeated calls / problems not solved); consultants used vs. employee driven improvements
Supply / value chain failures	Weak oversight driven by cost rather than value	Lower product costs being more than offset by higher administrative costs due to paperwork defects, rework, failures to deliver on time and others; savings not passed on by vendors
Target and goal setting	Excessive, meaningless and/or conflicting performance targets & KPIs drive adverse outcomes	Excess reporting / admin time; more meetings vs. voluntary collaboration and cooperation; workplace conflict / stress causing higher sick leave; excess management time resolving issues;
Behaviour and conduct	Individuals or small teams in one or more locations behave or act such that catastrophic organisational damage occurs	Non-compliance with regulations / fines; employee work duplicated vs. knowledge shared; privacy / confidentiality breaches cause higher legal costs; fraud / collusion between staff and with 3rd parties; need to rebuild image / brand marketing increases costs;

Systemic problems in the approach to pay are a well proven driver of perceived unfairness and can drive the wrong behavior (such as the Wells Fargo or Volkswagen examples). Knowledge and learning failures come

---

[22] All references to The Maturity Institute with permission

from a lack of collaboration and cooperation as well as higher turnover; one study[23] put this loss at $47 million per year per company. Failures in the supply chain, where a bias towards cost versus the relationship is predominant (an aspect of poor culture), can result in higher operating costs. Ineffective goal setting, where targets are handed down rather than being mutually agreed, also has negative impacts on employee behavior (again, the Wells Fargo situation but also many of the other underlying behavioral / ethical issues that were revealed behind the 2008 mortgages and toxic securities problems). The final example, related to behavior and conduct links back to the previous section on financial surprises.

Successful organizations used the COPQ framework developed by The American Society of Quality to extract the underlying costs and make then visible. Simplistically, the approach involves the identification of activities and events that occur in the organization that drive the consumption of resources, but which, if everything was working effectively, should not happen. A similar approach could be applied to the identification of existing operating costs that are being impacted by key risk areas in human governance and human capital management.

Traditional accounting systems lack many of the analytical approaches to reporting on these hidden costs. However, some might be developed by looking at HR reporting in areas like turnover and comparing current to "leading" practice and then applying a cost to the improvement opportunity. This might be done in several areas and will be explored more in the "Failure costs" discussion.

3.3 Missed opportunities.

The effective engagement of people in an organization not only results in lower operating costs, as just discussed, but also contributes to a higher level of innovation and creativity. This will drive both the opportunities to

---

[23] The Panopto Workplace Knowledge and Productivity Report, July 17, 2018.

improve current operations and, more importantly, the development of ideas to drive future growth.

Missed opportunity	Description of risk / impact
Limited continual improvement	Operational costs are not being continually reduced causing margin shrinkage; result is programs for cost reduction that often fail to remove the root cause of excess costs and lead to lowering of morale. The organization struggles to sustain a competitive advantage.
Limited innovation	Related to the above; lip service paid to new ideas from employees; feedback is slow or non-existent and managers / leaders do not actively encourage employee innovation. The result is a maturing of capability and offerings which can often only be resolved through mergers / acquisitions or the "buying in" of patents and product / service opportunities.
Limited ability to benefit from being "lean"	A lean organization is, by definition, one in which there are extremely low levels of waste; however, to "be lean" requires cooperation and collaboration across traditional functional organizational silos and a willingness of employees to take on more "caring and responsibility." Where people feel they are valued and recognized, the probability is that lean initiatives will bring greater positive results.

The above three items all relate to efforts around day-by-day improvements. Readers may reflect that one of the key competitive advantages of a company such as Toyota is in its ability to constantly improve everything that it does. This cannot be driven from the top by directive; it must be part of the ongoing interest; it must come from the interest, commitment, inquisitiveness, and creativity of the workforce together with their supervisors and others, who can collaborate to investigate and – where possible – implement new ideas.

Missed opportunity	Description of risk / impact
Responsiveness (market)	Organizations today seek to be agile and responsive. These qualities come from employees who care and are willing to collaborate, cooperate and communicate; in short, they are fully committed through what they do to the success of the business. A positive culture is one that creates this atmosphere; if these human qualities are not present, the organization will not attain the capability.
Responsive (change)	Organizations need to be able to respond rapidly to changing markets and deploy their changes as rapidly as possible. Effective leadership that fully embraces its human capital and creates a culture of trust and commitment will develop a foundation for rapid deployment of change rather than one where there is a lack of trust.
Responsive (regulatory)	For many organizations, the regulatory framework within which they operate holds the power to support (speed up) or frustrate (slow down) certain business initiatives and changes. An organization that has open and transparent communications with regulators and which builds trust in its commitment to behavior, compliance, and responsiveness will likely be better supported and trusted by regulators when changes are needed.

This second batch of opportunities arises from the ability to respond to change; this ability (once again driven by the behavior of people) has become a critical competitive advantage. The idea that "people do not like change," is inaccurate. What is true is that many people do not like to be told to change by others – such as management – especially when they have no understanding of the need for change, nor of the impact that it will have. A positive culture creates a higher level of confidence in management and enhances trust.

The author experienced a client example of this impact. A manufacturing plant based in Canada was part of a group of about forty plants in North America. This plant not only had one of the highest productivity levels but also seemed able to respond to schedule and product changes far faster and more effectively than any other plant. Additionally, based in Canada, it tended to have shorter production runs and more product changeovers than other, US-based operations that benefitted from greater specialization and larger volumes. An evaluation of why this difference occurred eventually revealed that the ONLY major difference was the level of trust and respect the employees held for both the General Manager and for people in supervisory roles.

It is worth mentioning as a codicil to this story that the General Manager was also one of the longest serving managers, who had been with the company almost his entire career and had therefore had the time to develop strong relationships. The practice of changing managers and appointing people who have little hands-on experience with the work being managed can, in itself, have a negative impact on culture.

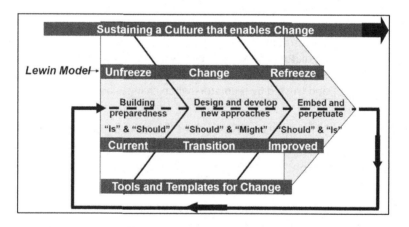

Responsiveness is a critical success factor and organizations that develop a "change-ready" culture gain a strong competitive advantage. While many ideas and resources are available on the "tools and templates for change", it is harder to find those for managing the impact of change on the human dimension. Change takes place within an envelope of organizational activity and reality and, while a change initiative is an event often managed as a project, the people involved are part of an organizational continuum. Change readiness comes from this continuum, which is why good change management initiatives involve an assessment of organizational readiness as part of their preparation, and why organizations with positive cultures re often more "change ready" allowing the projects to proceed faster.

The final examples of lost opportunity are driven by human behavior – individual or collective:

Missed opportunity	Description of risk / impact
Reputation loss	While purchase decisions are heavily financially based, increasingly products are not differentiated, and the " ability to do business with the company – i.e., the interactions between staff and clients – becomes a key competitive edge. In this case, a positive reputation through staff who are knowledgeable, and care becomes an asset in retaining clients and growing sales.
Talent attraction	In many knowledge-based companies, attraction and retention of human talent is a core requirement. Creating a reputation generated by existing employees as a "great place to work" will assist in the attraction of potential talent (especially in a competitive market where people have choices), as well as reducing the costs of hiring.
Investor attraction	Investors are becoming increasingly concerned with organizational behavior as it relates to the risk of their investment (both capital and returns). Organizations that develop, sustain, and communicate positive attributes that are seen to lower risk will have less challenge attracting investors and will possibly pay less of a financial risk premium for the money that they borrow.

Reputation loss can come from an organization that collectively fails to change with the times and, as a result, becomes out of touch with the social reality of the world within which it operates. The value of an organization's brand or reputation can be significant, yet it is not part of financial reporting. This area of reputation is important, as **environmental, social and governance (ESG)** reporting is demanded by investors and is becoming more mainstream. Failure to address societal concerns about *environmental* impacts can cause surprises (some of the fines and scandals mentioned earlier occurred in this area). They can also cause people to become disenchanted with the way an organization behaves and thus seek alternative products, services, and suppliers. *Social* awareness, the issue about relationships with society as a whole, as well as between people both internally and externally, is important to reputation. Organizations are beginning to understand that, as part of their "license to operate," they need to consider the impact of their actions on people both within and outside the organization. What is critical is that organizational culture that is founded on its responses to both environmental and social issues is a core component of its *governance* – how the organization is managed and led.

Attraction and retention of human talent is another key competitive advantage and one which is enhanced when an organization positions itself as a "preferred employer." The pool of available people with the skills and capabilities required may have choices, and candidates are more selective than they used to be. Some will look at the culture as more important than the salary and will accept lower compensation to start work with an organization that they have greater respect for. The hiring organization MUST be socially connected to be able to respond effectively to these candidates.

Finally, culture will have an impact on the investors – mainly because of the issue of risk. Many investors are becoming more mature in their understanding of the factors underlying financial performance. Investment advisors are also expanding their analytical services to seek out information about aspects of organizations that make them more aware of issues such as ESG reporting. This has already been demonstrated by shareholder activism in areas such as executive compensation that was discussed earlier. There are many areas of hidden opportunity that can all be leveraged by building a positive culture.

3.4   SMEs, culture, and costs

Before we leave this chapter, it is important to address the significant number of organizations that are NOT large or publicly traded. The examples given so far may tend to suggest that this problem only applies to big organizations, but hidden costs exist everywhere.

- Culture in a smaller organizations is often managed by the attitudes of the owner and the degree to which they are involved with the grass roots of the business and know what is going on. They should already know where the risk and problems are and have addressed them.
- If the owner of a smaller business has a leadership style that engages and involves employees and has (almost) eliminated fear in the workplace, these employees will know where the problems are and, given the opportunity, will offer improvement suggestions.
- As a business grows in employee numbers, the problems may start to become overlooked as the owner is no longer able to be close to the action. This is where a culture needs to start being built to encourage the continuing identification of problems and opportunities.

3.5   Hidden costs – summary

Whether we consider the hidden 90% of the iceberg from the "gold in the mine" concept, or the hidden costs approach, we know that there are opportunities to improve organizational performance. The problem is that, unless you know where the waste or unappreciated opportunity is, there is little you can do about it. Successful strategies have been employed by CEOs for many years to counteract this lack of information. Management, by walking around, building a culture that allows people to raise ideas and speak their mind, or just doing what they think based on their experience, are taking the right action. In some cases, this involves constant shake-ups and reorganization of business. This can be self-defeating in that, unless people understand the purpose, they tend to watch from the sidelines.

For too many years, organizations have given lip service to the phrase "people are our most important asset," yet often actual management of human capital as a strategic resource continues to focus on people as costs rather than investments. Financial reporting often masks the impact that poor human capital management has on an organization's actual performance, as well as its potential opportunity to reduce risk and enhance value creation. Understanding of the impact of human behavior has been downplayed and often referred to as the "soft and fuzzy" side of management, yet the growing importance of organizational culture is encouraging investors and leaders to take the issue of human behavior and the optimization of human capital more seriously.

Because the impacts of poor, or less than optimum, approaches to human capital management are not clearly demonstrated through financial reporting, Investors, boards, and CEOs often fail to grasp the significance of a strategic focus around human-centric strategy and the benefits it can bring; short-term incentives add to the focus on short-term performance that often exacerbates the challenge of shifting focus.

There is a financial risk to a less-than-optimum human-centric strategy; at worst, this can expose the organization to higher operating costs, including unplanned and unanticipated financial impacts such as penalties and fines; for most organizations, even at the medium and lower risk rankings, there remains an opportunity to reduce hidden costs and enhance strategic competitive capability. As a business grapples with the need for competitive advantage, transparency, and sustainability, the adoption of additional measures that focus on whole-system performance becomes a necessary imperative.

Where are the costs of poor culture hiding? Summary

- People's behavior has a direct impact on the success and sustainability of any organization.
- Without a strategically driven, clearly defined culture people's behavior will be unpredictable.
- If culture is not managed, based on values and expectations, there is a risk of a poor culture developing.
- If a poor culture exists, the three cost impacts will be financial surprises, hidden costs, and lost opportunities.
- Corporate culture is core to systems thinking and can bring substantial performance improvements, if applied.
- Surprises can be caused by misunderstanding expectations, failure of controls or illegal / unethical behavior.
- Hidden costs are buried within operating costs and are largely invisible yet might be significant.
- A five-stage approach of uncertainty, awakening, enlightenment, wisdom, and certainty will help the learning process.
- Like an iceberg, most of the costs of poor quality are hidden.
- The impact of disengaged employees can cost businesses billions annually.
- Significant performance improvements can be seen when the causes of poor culture are removed.

Checklist
• Has your organizational culture evolved, or has it been defined and managed?
• Does your organization have a defined set of values upon which expected individual and group behavior is based?
• Are these values deployed throughout the organization?
• Are the values aligned with policies, procedures, and leadership development?
• Does your organization experience any financial surprises?
• Is your financial performance a continuing challenge?
• Are there indicators that your workforce may be disengaged?
• Do you ever discover costs that are being incurred that could have been avoided through improved communication, collaboration, or cooperation?
• Do you have problems at the supervisory or leadership level where employee disputes are escalated?
• Are relationships with suppliers and customers on a win / win continuous improving foundation?
• Do you believe you are getting the best from your workforce in terms of innovation, creativity, and commitment?
• Do you have HR metrics that are being used that link directly back to financial performance (e.g., costed turnover)?

4 A framework for understanding

Most accounting systems fail to provide an understanding of the impact of a negative or positive culture within an organization – yet, intuitively, we know that opportunities and benefits or excess costs exist when the issue of culture is not addressed. In most cases, human behavior is at the center of an organization's culture, so if an organization is to invest in initiatives to better understand and encourage positive behavior, it will tend to only do so if it understands the impact of NOT doing anything.

This approach to understanding the COPC concept is based on ideas developed in the early days of quality management when those involved were having trouble gaining management commitment to investing in quality improvement initiatives, especially process improvements. Looking back, organizations have recognized that, far from it being an additional cost or burden, investing to achieve high quality significantly reduced costs and improved many facets of organizational competitiveness. Those who failed to understand this have disappeared.

As time has passed, management has learned about poor quality, and process improvements have been initiated and deployed in most organizations so that high quality is the norm. It is now becoming increasingly realized that the next challenge is to optimize the value of human capital – but once again the challenge is in justifying the investments and approaches required. The technical committee TC 176 of the International Standards Organization, who oversee the quality management series of standards, is now developing a guideline to support the importance of culture. Another ISO working group, TC 260, who are working on standards for human resources management, has also recently developed a technical specification for addressing organizational culture - ISO/TS 24178:2021.

The following framework will help management start to understand the impact of hidden costs and opportunities related to human capital and organizational culture. Failures, are the problems and lost opportunities while prevention and assessment are the investment required to eliminate root causes and "change the way we do things:"

Cost classification	Color code	Description
Prevention costs	**GREEN** Good costs	Spending that contributes to eliminate or avoid excess costs caused by poor culture – can be considered investments in building capability and reducing unplanned costs.
Assessment costs	**AMBER** Take care	Spending required to evaluate, assess, and sustain a positive culture.
Failure costs – internal	**RED** All these areas are costs to be avoided	Excess and unnecessary spending caused by a negative culture that impacts the organization internally
Failure costs – external		Excess and unnecessary spending caused by a negative culture that impacts the organization externally including impacts on suppliers and customers, clients, brand value and others
Failure costs – strategic		Lost opportunities to enhance competitive advantage caused by poor culture including impacts from lost input and ideas from employees, customers, clients, community, and others

The challenge for organizations is to ask themselves whether these costs and lost opportunities exist today and, if so, where they are and what the impact is. For most organizations, all the costs of failure are buried in today's operating expenses and are invisible in terms of their specific driver or cause – but they are there. The result is continual efforts to drive down costs through traditional approaches, such as headcount reductions or added pressure on suppliers, and even selling price increases in the marketplace – none of which will address the root causes and build a sustainable business model.

These "reactive" responses to cost cutting, further worsen the buried costs of a poor culture and thwart the ability to exploit opportunities through innovation and creativity. Real improvement can only come from addressing and eliminating the poor culture itself; these efforts will be strategic and will take time – but understanding the hidden opportunities to reduce costs and enhance competitiveness should help management justify the investments in time and resources required.

As a final note, risk management practitioners will see a relationship to their activity here. Failure costs occur when controls fail to work; assessment or appraisal costs are what you spend to monitor and manage those risks that you cannot eliminate, and prevention costs are those activities that you invest in to identify, eliminate, or control risks. Thus, a **costs of culture analysis** provides a financial picture of governance and risk management relative to problems related to behavior.

Prevention costs No one wants to spend money without understanding what the payback is, and because there is little understanding of the costs of a poor culture, many of the investments necessary to reduce such problems are either minimized or avoided. This is all about changing the system to remove root causes so that the symptoms and underlying problems disappear. Additionally, when people problems occur, the action is often event driven and fails to seek the root cause which is systemic.

Prevention costs are referred to as "investments" because they put in place structures and systems that establish a human-centric approach, in which everything that impacts people and relationships is considered strategic. The process starts with the governance framework that asks the questions: What type of organization do we want to be? and What type of framework for ensuring maximum engagement of the workforce do we need to put in place?

While many organizations establish their governance frameworks with compliance in mind, progressive investors and boards recognize that they need to add to these minimum requirements. As an example, this would include knowing what underpins the brand image that must be understood and sustained. In the model discussed earlier, the costs of poor culture occur in five stages:

	Description	Prevention
1	Uncertainty	Costs minimized or eliminated – limited value
2	Awakening	Costs minimized – value understood
3	Enlightenment	Start of investment – linked to failures
4	Wisdom	Continued investment – failures plus opportunity
5	Certainty	Strategic – clear systemwide ROI from HRM

Investments in prevention start to be more fully understood when the real cost of failures has been identified, either through actual cost impacts or from a risk assessment that identifies the need for investment in HR management as an approach to behavior-based assurance of expectations. Typically, once an organization starts to understand behavioral failures, and develops an understanding of root causes, cash flow will tend to be directed more towards prevention areas that are soon offset by an ROI from lower failure costs. Finally, prevention costs are considered "Green" costs because they are "good" costs and reflect money that is an investment in reduced risk of failure. (Traditionally, without an understanding of the cost of failure, prevention costs are seen as overheads and are minimized to the greatest degree possible).

Appraisal costs These are considered "Amber" costs as, in a perfect world, where all policies and procedures are followed and no unexpected behavior is possible, these costs could be eliminated, but that is not the reality. A minimum set of activities is usually required to ensure that the system is working - these might be considered the control aspects of the response to risk management. (In an enlightened organization these costs and prevention, form a core part of internal controls).

Because people's behavior – a key aspect of organizational culture – occurs in every instance of an interaction, both internally and externally, effective prevention as well as appraisal must cover all aspects. This requires internal activities to ensure supervisor-to-subordinate and peer-to-peer interactions both within and between work areas are included. External relationships with suppliers, clients / customers, and a variety of others where relationships are a key asset, would also require planning and monitoring.

	Description	Appraisal
1	Uncertainty	Costs minimized – seen as control of staff
2	Awakening	Costs minimized – value understood
3	Enlightenment	Start or shift in investment – linked to failures
4	Wisdom	Continued investment – failures plus opportunity
5	Certainty	Strategic – clear systemwide ROI from HRM

The cost profile is similar to that of prevention, in that there is an "Aha!" moment when the need for information, usually approached differently from traditional HR surveys, is seen as critical both to enhance the quality of the culture and to ensure optimum employee engagement. One key issue is that by stages four and five, people's input becomes increasingly critical – not just to maximize current productivity but to develop ways in which human capital can provide greater strategic value to the business.

Failure costs are grouped under three categories, each of which has a different impact on the organization:

- **External failures**. These are problems that occur either after a product or service has been delivered to the client, or elsewhere "outside" the workplace.
- **Internal failures**. These are problems that occur in the workplace, and typically are invisible to clients.
- **Strategic failures**. These are lost opportunities that exist because of either delays in responding or a lack of response.

There is no need for a hard-and-fast rule for each category so long as "the cost of failure" can be identified. These costs are also often quite difficult to determine; users should worry somewhat less about the exact accuracy of the numbers rather than the need to identify where failures are occurring and the relative impact on the business.

	Description	Failure
1	Uncertainty	Significant unknown cost impacts
2	Awakening	Start of identification of obvious costs
3	Enlightenment	Employee engagements identifies more costs
4	Wisdom	Costs being identified and reported
5	Certainty	Improved culture leading to growth opportunity

At the stage of uncertainty (Stage 1), there is little understanding of where money is being wasted due to poor culture; surprises can occur, and costs are buried, creating performance problems. Some failure costs may be easy to observe, such as fines and penalties, and this might be the start of Stage 2 – awakening. However, many costs will be hidden as part of the "cost of doing business;" these will need to be identified and the events costed so that the impact can be extracted from the other costs that reflect the ongoing operational costs.

As one moves from *Enlightenment* to *Wisdom* and *Certainty*, additional buried costs will come to light as employees identify additional events that can be traced back to a poor culture. As trust starts to develop, employees will be encouraged to identify additional opportunities where a lack of engagement has been leading to knowledge not being shared.

For human-centric organizations, behavior-based values rank equally to corporate purpose. Human behavior is as critically important at the planning and strategy level as is the focus on task-based goals and objectives. This parallel approach requires that the values established to guide "the way things are done" become an equal part of the organization's business model. The COPC approach reflects the allocation of resources that occurs as part of the business model in the same way that "Purpose" is translated into processes and activities for execution (i.e., "Do.").

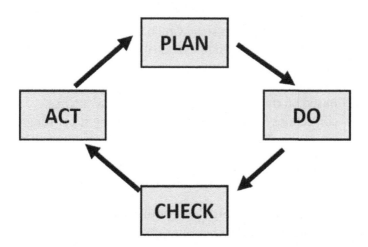

This holistic approach to embedding behavioral aspects of organizational activity into every aspect of the business model is the sign of a truly human-centric approach, where the human aspects become equal to the "purpose" aspects and are embedded at every stage - planning, execution, measuring and monitoring and planned action.

Plan	Governance-driven: defines desired behavior built on a set of values. Behavioral risk assessment determines *prevention costs / investments* required. Planning incurs prevention costs to establish policy and procedures and investment required for "control" purposes to prevent problems. Includes all HR operational process planning.
Do	Plans are executed: the "what" driven by goals and objectives and the "how" driven by expected behaviors. Leadership and management of people, and interaction driven by values / culture following human-centric policy and procedure, and leadership climate. As "Do" is executed, *failure costs* will occur where actual behavior does not meet planned expectations.
Check	Constant use of metrics to assess behavioral / climate / culture performance; includes checks required as part of *appraisal costs*. This stage would also include internal process metrics used to assess HR processes as being "in control."
Act	Based on the check data, actions taken as "course corrections" through mentoring, coaching supporting, retraining. This could be part of either prevention or failure costs.

This system wide approach will provide a foundation for a definition of the cost of culture equivalent to the cost of quality that was discussed earlier - that might read as follows:

> **Definition**
> The cost of culture is the difference between what an organizations actual costs and performance are, and what these might be, if every aspect of human activity and interaction was working at the optimum level.

The next chapters focus on each of the main cost areas described in this chapter, and identify specific types of activities and events that fall into each category. Following that, a process for starting an action plan is outlined to help identify the problems with a poor culture, extract the costs and start making changes so that employee engagement can be applied leading to enhanced "bottom line" performance.

Building a framework for understanding, summary
• Traditional accounting provides little understanding of the cost of culture – good or bad.
• There are three different types of costs related to the management of culture – prevention, appraisal and failure.
• Prevention costs are investments, mainly in people-related activities, that are aimed at creating a positive culture.
• Appraisal costs are expenses incurred in ensuring that a positive culture is being maintained.
• Failure costs are those costs that should not be incurred if the culture is positive and fully enables high performance.
• Failure costs can be internal or external and are often related to unnecessary labor expenses.
• In a poor culture, there are also "lost opportunities" that are like failure costs.
• Failure costs are largely hidden, and the costs involved are usually unknown or under-estimated.
• Prevention, appraisal, and failure costs can all be mapped on to the stages in the PDCA business model.
• The planning and management of desired behavior mirror the framework for planning and managing desired purpose.

Checklist
• Are you aware of the financial impacts of a poor culture?
• Do you have visibility into culture-related costs, including your investments (prevention and appraisal) and failures (both internal and external)?
• Are you calculating an ROI from the prevention costs that are being incurred based on reducing failures?
• Where are you in the five-point scale of cost awareness – Uncertain? Awakening? Enlightened? Wise? Certain?
• Is your business model (such as PDCA) inclusive of both task and behavior aspects?

5 Prevention costs

Costs of poor culture – Prevention costs
Prevention costs are investments that are made to fund activities that are specifically designed to create and sustain a positive culture. Examples include planning for human capital; design and development of HR systems and structures that support engagement; design of leadership and other development programs; design and development of communications frameworks

Prevention costs include spending that contributes to eliminate excess costs caused by poor culture. The problem for many organizations is that most of these costs are seen as overheads which are bad and should therefore be reduced wherever possible. Failing to invest adequately in these areas will lead to several types of failure costs – some seen, some unseen. While the HR function has traditionally had responsibility for "people issues," its funding has often been driven by compliance in areas such as health and safety and, more lately, diversity. HR is also funded for process management to perform the activities required to obtain people with the necessary skills, qualities, and experience for operational needs.

A key challenge is that while HR supports the people needs of the business, it does not manage or lead the people on a day-to-day basis. This isolated approach to HR management leads to the assumption that anything to do with improving culture is the responsibility of HR. Not only is that untrue, but it is also impossible. The greatest factors that impact culture are established by the governance framework within which management operates. This framework must see people as a strategic asset that is critical to value creation and enterprise sustainability. The following would typically be prevention costs:

Prevention cost	Aspects of the governance framework
Governance foundation	Costs of working with board to develop a strategic statement of organizational values to guide behavior and interactions with all stakeholders; development of board oversight for key operational roles (e.g., committees, areas of oversight responsibility, and accountability, reporting, delegation of authority). Linkage to societal <IR> and SDG goals
Strategic focus	Development of organizational purpose that embraces the needs of all key stakeholders and focuses on societal outcomes (purpose focuses on task, values focus on behavior)
Compliance design	Review, understanding and strategy for compliance with all requirements from key stakeholders (e.g., regulators, legal, financial, safety) and development of overall governance and control framework
Client input	Costs associated with strategic interaction with clients and other stakeholders, to align organizational behavior with stakeholder expectations, including brand / reputation linkages
Organizational design and business model	Development of a business model defining key inputs (including multiple capitals) and their deployment in organizational value creation and development; identification of key roles and responsibilities that align with both outcome and behavioral expectations (values)

How people are to be treated (in other words, led and managed) has to be established as a core principle through the development of a set of values.

To be effective, HR needs the right climate to be defined and upheld by the whole leadership and management function. Based on this concept, prevention costs are often at the whole organization level – not just HR; this might be thought of as the "crucible" within which everything takes place.

This first segment illustrates the types of cost that are associated with making organizational culture a strategic, governance issue. Owners and investors are becoming increasingly concerned about the risk associated with unexpected behavior that leads to fines, penalties, fraud, and other conduct that reflects badly on the organization as being "socially responsible." Thus, leadership to make this change must at the governance level. This is the direction to management by the board, to deploy resources into areas that generate competitive advantage and are core to value creation, (and it requires looking beyond compliance). Some key aspects of prevention investment would include:

Prevention cost	Description
Communication design	Development of programs and frameworks for ensuring compliant and transparent communications internally and externally
Values alignment	Development of stated values into specific operational expectations around decision making within all key activities and functions and embedding these in performance criteria (the "is" / "is not" structure)
Strategic alignment	Costs associated with development of strategic plans that align organizational goals and objectives with stated purpose, mission, and values
Aspects / impact review	Assessment of business model for determination of aspects and impacts of organizational value creation and development of sustainable / minimum footprint
HR design	Development of processes, procedures and frameworks that ensure people management approaches reflect organizational values

Prevention cost	Description
Leadership design	Development of leadership framework – criteria, development, evaluation
Supply chain policy	Development of standards and performance for the selection and strategic alignment with external third parties balancing both relationships and continual improvement
Operational alignment	Costs associated with the development of corporate policies, procedures, and processes to ensure they align with behavioral expectations (mapping process to values)
Performance management design	Development of aligned set of organizational metrics that decompose both purpose and values into operational activity and outcome metrics; includes areas such as service standards development. Alignment with hiring, orientation, training and development and compensation approaches

The next area of prevention costs would be funding applied to "operationalizing" the intended direction established at the governance level. This is where intent becomes converted into execution. Many organizations establish some level of people focus at the board / governance level, but failure often occurs because the intent never becomes part of the reality of day-to-day operations and interaction.

As can be seen from the above examples, behavioral aspects must be woven through every aspect of relationship building. How people are treated by HR activities and support, and other operational systems; how leaders are trained to lead people with behavior that reflects the values that underpin the desired culture; the development of policies towards clients and suppliers – based on ensuring that positive relationship development ranks equally with other commercial issues.

These aspects of prevention are about investing in all aspects of the business where human behavior, from the need to collaborate, cooperate, and communicate through to making decisions, must reflect the "way things are done" so that the desired culture becomes the way of life.

Prevention cost	Description
Talent acquisition and evaluation	Develop a strategy for hiring "the right people" including underlying tools and processes
HR process alignment	Design and development of HR processes and support systems that align with values, including benefits, health and safety, diversity, and inclusion
Compensation design	Development and design of compensation systems that balance shared rewards with strategic and sustainable outcomes and reflect organizational values
Training, and development	Costs associated with the development of materials and programs that ensure full awareness and understanding of organizational purpose, behaviors, and outcomes for all employees

The final aspect of prevention costs involves ensuring that key aspects of the underpinning HR systems and processes are human-centric and reflect the desired values of the organization. Simple examples would be to ensure that the impact of personality was understood at the time of hiring, (not for "typing" but to assess the candidate's alignment with the organizations values and behavioral expectations). This ensures that candidates complement the core culture, and that orientation or on-boarding is seen to be as important as safety training, rather than being done "as and when time allows."

A risk assessment is an essential aspect of ensuring that prevention costs (and appraisal costs) are driven by possible causes of failure – they are, after all, investments to mitigate the risk of failures occurring. More mature organizations may be using tools such as human factor risk assessments as part of their health and safety approach. While these are a somewhat new development, they have evolved from a tool known as a **Failure Mode and Effect Analysis (FMEA)** that was developed and applied during the quality and process revolution. An FMEA is a structured approach to evaluating every step in a particular work process to assess the risk of failures and to determine whether changes to the process or additional controls might reduce the probability of failures. This thinking has been applied to non-manufacturing organizations such as NASA, who have developed a hybrid approach – referred to as **Human-Factors FMEA (HF-FMEA)**. The key types of questions in FMEA include:

- What is the process and the underlying activities, events, and tasks?
- At each step what is the risk of an error occurring?
- How serious might this error be if it occurs?
- What is the potential number of occurrences?
- What controls are currently in place to mitigate the risk of failure?
- Are current controls adequate or should additional checks (investment) be made?

This linkage between risk assessment and controls, as it applies to organizational activity, has shifted towards human behavior as the service economy has developed. While it is beyond the scope of this book to explore human factor risk assessments, the evolution of thinking around potential human behaviors in certain situations will clearly evolve as organizations strive for a greater understanding of culture. The better an organization knows and understands the root causes behind potential behavioral failures, the more effectively the governance approach will be – ensuring adequate controls are in place to mitigate such risks. Human behavior is extremely complex, and people do not always act in a rational or predictable manner. Developing control frameworks that take this into account will be part of future strategic success; investing in prevention costs will be a core part of this.

Prevention costs can be considered the foundations of understanding the concept of cost related to creating a positive culture, being one where human capital is considered as a prime driver of organizational value creation and retention. Culture is not an HR issue but an organizational challenge; because it is strategic, it transcends the functional aspects of organizational design and must be integral to the mosaic of how the different parts of the business model or system are integrated. Performance is a composite of the results of all resources employed by management being optimized for their highest level of potential. This thinking must be designed into every aspect of organizational activity, starting above the level of functional accountability, and then being deployed into and within all areas of activity.

Cultures will form without this happening, but they will not be predictable, nor will they reflect any strategic intent that aligns with the corporate purpose or the sustaining of reputation, capability, and therefore value. The application of the underlying principles, defined by the values, must be seen again and again – reinforced by actions from leaders in all departments – and they must be seen both internally and externally.

Prevention costs, summary
• Prevention costs are strategic investments in policies, procedures, systems, and training to build a positive culture.
• Prevention costs are driven by the steps required to put in place human aspects of governance and risk management.
• Many organizations are spending this money but are unaware of the ROI aspect, because failure is not known.
• Because of the unknown failures, prevention costs are often seen as overhead costs to be minimized.
• Prevention costs include both areas of HR spending and other costs driven by a strategic approach to culture.
• Prevention costs can be incurred internally and externally, can include assessment services and other third-party support.
• Prevention costs occur throughout the organization – from board governance to all employees and suppliers.
• Many prevention costs are incurred as part of the hiring process, getting the right people on board.

Checklist
• What prevention costs are currently being incurred and how are they reported?
• Is there an understanding of the expected ROI or cost avoidance through making "culture" investments?
• Are the prevention investments being driven by an effective assessment of the strategic risk from an unmanaged culture?
• Has a human factors risk assessment been carried out beyond those for health and safety?
• Has a human factors risk analysis been carried out, to determine prevention investments as they relate to establishing the desired behavior from people and relationships?
• Does the board see the prevention costs as investments necessary for human capital governance?
• Have all aspects of human interaction been risk assessed to determine prevention cost requirements?

The Cost of Poor Culture

6 Appraisal costs

Costs of poor culture – Appraisal costs
Appraisal costs are continuing repetitive costs incurred to measure and monitor the human capital aspect of organizational resources and the various systems to ensure they continue to operate effectively. This would include surveys and other feedback approaches both internally and externally; compliance audits relative to employee well-being; all testing and assessments at time of hiring; exit interviews

Appraisal costs include spending that is required to evaluate, assess, and sustain a positive culture; these are typically on-going "sustaining" costs that are necessary to ensure the continuity of a positive culture. Many of these costs are considered overheads and, as such, are typically subject to scrutiny and minimization wherever possible.

Failure to invest at an adequate level in this type of expenditure will ultimately lead to failure costs. There may be a belief that the culture "has been fixed" because preventative actions have been taken, and that sustaining costs can now be reduced, but this can potentially increase the risk of a positive culture declining over time. These costs are critical to ensure a robust and sustainable culture is maintained.

Appraisal costs may be identified as such or may be buried and hidden within other costs related to broader or different activities. At the core of an organization's culture is a common way of engaging, communicating, cooperating, and otherwise interacting during day-to-day activity. Anyone who is brought into this process as a new employee, supplier, or contractor, whether part-time, temporary, or other resource, will have an impact on others. Therefore, a central theme of sustaining the culture is to **manage entry** and this forms the first group of suggested appraisal costs. It includes people who become leaders within the culture, to ensure that no one in a leadership position is given that responsibility unless their actions and beliefs align with the corporate values.

The list below provides an example of the costs associated with cultural sustainability, although it should be considered as a base and/or starting point for discussion.

Appraisal cost	Description
Hiring	Costs associated with identification, evaluation, and selection of employees to ensure that they align with anticipated requirements of both technical competency and behavioral / values expectations
Orientation	Costs associated with ensuring that all new hires are fully aware of their relationships, responsibilities, and expectations
Leadership development	Costs associated with the selection and promotion of all managers / leaders to ensure their capability to sustain both task outcomes and expected behaviors and values
Supplier selection and development	All costs associated with supplier selection and building the initial relationship

This list would also depend upon the type of business; as an example, a distributor selected to sell the products or services would be seen as acting on behalf of the product manufacturer and would therefore have an impact on the manufacturer's reputation; thus selecting a distributor that "aligns" with the manufacturers culture that stands behind its' brand and reputation would be important. The same might be true for contractors or other service suppliers; for example, many organizations outsource much of their post-sales support to third parties and these would need to be vetted for relationship capability as well as technical skills.

Whilst it is almost impossible to evaluate and approve customers for their cultural alignment, it is important to realize that this can be a key area of "cultural clash"; for example, if the client has no time for any relationship and just wants to focus on the lowest price, caring little about any other needs for collaboration, then this must at least be recognized and understood.

Appraisal cost	Description
Cultural audit	Costs associated with internal and external reviews of actual to planned behavioral aspects of business activity
Risk assessment	Costs associated with regular review, evaluation, and action to manage enterprise risks across all capitals including human aspects
Feedback / evaluation	Costs associated with the continual feedback among all stakeholders on actual vs. expected performance (e.g., 360° for managers); also surveys and feedback from all other key stakeholders; includes customer and other stakeholder feedback
Investor / regulator engagement	Associated with sustaining outreach and proactive interaction with key stakeholders to ensure their expectations and evaluation of performance are being understood and responded to
Supplier calibration	Performance reviews, problem solving, joint development initiatives, etc.

Appraisal cost	Description
Employee review and support	Time spent by managers in coaching, supporting, guiding, and developing employees

The next set of appraisal costs might include any types of checks, measurements, and periodic assessments that take place to evaluate whether the system of "culture sustaining" activities, continues to work effectively. Focusing on one traditional area – that of employee surveys – it is important that the traditional approach of long, in-depth, periodic assessments is not seen as the one to use. Culture can vary depending upon many situations and a regular "health check" is more important. There are many available and developing real-time assessment tools that can provide this type of information; the key is that are fast and focused so as to quickly spot emerging shifts.

One especially important aspect is that generic questions must be the minority; what an organization needs to know as part of its assessment activity is whether the _desired behavior_ is being demonstrated. The only way to do this is to develop question sets that are based on the behaviors expected as defined in the organization's own values.

This third area of appraisal costs might include costs associated with taking action to sustain the system capability that are, therefore, not part of normal operational costs. One might argue that some of these are prevention costs but, once again, this list should be used to provoke discussion and ideas rather than be seen as an absolute list. Using the concepts applied in quality management, where calibration costs related to sustaining the accuracy of key equipment being used in operational processes are considered appraisal costs, these types of expense that help keep people "on track" should arguably also be part of the appraisal.

Appraisal cost	Description
Private counselling	Costs associated with providing EAP and equivalent resources to ensure the well-being of all employees, and support where needed
Collaborative investment	Ongoing costs related to time involved for inter-departmental team projects and activity including shift overlaps, joint task force, KAIZEN teams / CI teams, etc. Costs associated with supporting continual improvement and organizational learning
Safety / health	Costs associated with collaborative efforts to ensure a safe and healthy workplace, and actions required to meet commitments beyond minimum compliance
Team / collaboration development	Costs associated with the development of collaboration and cooperation between different stakeholders and departments, including team development activities

At this stage in building and managing an organizational culture, the more appropriate question might be: Which items on the above list are not being invested in or are being inadequately funded? This might then lead to a review of the failure costs (covered in the next chapters) and evaluation of whether any of the unplanned costs of buried expenses are due to the absence of some of these sustaining activities.

Appraisal costs, summary
• Appraisal costs are associated with ensuring the desired culture and "human environment" is operating as planned.
• Appraisal costs include surveys, assessments, and other tools.
• Appraisal can also include one-on-one assessments.
• Approaches to appraisal form the basis of "Check" in the Plan, Do, Check, Act management model.
• The metrics adopted at the Check stage must include both "whole system climate" (i.e., culture) measures, and HR process and outcome measures.
Checklist
• Are the appraisal investments driven by understanding where risk occur and what needs to be checked?
• Is there adequate information from appraisal results that provides confidence in whole-system effectiveness and compliance?
• Are the climate checks based on specific criteria (questions) that mirror the expectations based on values (and not generic)?
• Do the appraisal results indicate that the desired behaviors are being modelled at all interactions (internal, inter-departmental, external and others)?

7 Failure costs – internal

> ***Costs of poor culture – Internal failure costs***
> Internal failure costs result from behavior not conforming to expectations and requirements within the organization, and not directly being observed, or recognized as impacting on external stakeholders, such as suppliers, customers, and other third parties.

The first and most critical aspect of internal failure costs is excess (and unnecessary) spending that is caused by a negative culture that impacts the organization internally. While some of these costs might be already seen and reported on as separate expense items, such as legal fees for unplanned terminations, or arbitration costs, many remain buried within other areas of operating costs.

Internal failure costs are typically only visible within the organization; in particular, they have a large impact on employee productivity and output but, unfortunately, this cannot be seen from traditional financial reporting – all management knows is that costs are too high relative to outcomes. Being able to identify events that are occurring and generating a demand for resources is an important starting point in understanding the excess costs of a poor culture.

Because most internal failure costs are buried in existing expenses, there needs to be a concerted effort to try and extract these events when they occur; without this, management "does not know what it does not know." (We will discuss how you develop and implement an action plan in Chapter 10.) In many of these events, identifying what is happening and what sorts of costs are involved is more important that knowing the cost with 100% accuracy.

One of the best ways to identify wastage is by asking those people involved in the day-to-day activities of the business. The types of events that occur if the culture is less than optimum is listed below. Those familiar with the costs of poor quality will see some level of similarity because processes may be the root cause – but they cannot be fixed because of lack of employee engagement.

Internal failure cost	Description
Lateness and absenteeism	Costs associated with unplanned absence from work
Sickness and sick leave	Unplanned / higher than normal costs associated with sick time off in particular areas, such as disability and stress-based leave (would include overtime costs for replacement workers and impact on deliveries)
Turnover (hiring)	Costs associated with hiring, orienting, and developing new employees at a higher-than-normal turnover level
Turnover (productivity)	Costs associated with lower levels of productivity; higher rejects; failures; complaints associated with a higher-than-average level of newer / short-term employees
Firing / termination losses	Costs associated with unplanned firings and terminations due to behavior inconsistent with stated values
Excess overtime / premium	Costs incurred when problems, delays, and demotivation resulting in process delays which are then corrected through overtime work
Compensation /benefits	Higher premiums paid for various insurance plans, including workplace compensation premiums due to poor experience records
Legal	Excess costs incurred relative to internal problem resolution, including situations such as dismissal without due cause (poor leadership); costs associated with problem escalation – often in a unionized workplace

These first items may be reported as HR statistics but are often not costed in terms of their impact; additionally, there may be an opportunity to establish a benchmark "normal" level (of turnover, for example) and to cost any that fall over or under this benchmark level as a failure. However, this is *not* recommended as it distracts from the fact that *any loss is a cost to the organization*. A better approach would be to cost the total losses and then display them on a control chart, so that the total impact can be seen.

Internal failure cost	Description
Casual / contract	Additional costs incurred to manage workload when internal cooperation and collaboration are causing delays and backlogs that can only be covered by temporary staffing
Investigation	Costs associated with problem solving for unplanned incidents and failures including investigation and corrective action
Safety losses	Excess caused through unsafe work practices caused by lack of protection, training, or excessive focus on output over employee welfare
Meetings / problem resolution	Excess labor costs and delays created when issues have to be escalated and resolved by managers, as employees are unwilling to take risk of collaborating (results in delays, meetings, etc.)
Collaborative losses	Excess costs (labor typically) due to employees having to wait or not receiving support from other departments (silo impact); includes failure to communicate updates and changes
Premium penalties	Excess costs due to lack of collaboration, cooperation, information sharing, etc. resulting in process delays and items, e.g. documents, being sent by courier
Control loss	Costs associated with a higher level of internal controls due to assessed risk from lack of trust with employees

The next segment also primarily concerns labor costs that are incurred and buried within the overall expense reporting. There are several costs that result from a lack of cooperation and collaboration; not only do things take longer and therefore require more staff to meet deadlines, or additional costs such as overtime and employment of contract staff, but there is also a potential impact on other aspects, such as client loss. Some of these items may again be hard to cost but the opportunity to identify the relevant events can help focus the need to manage the culture. One classic type of cost that might be seen here is due to the decision to outsource a particular activity because the department that needs it finds it easier to deal with an external organization than seek support internally.

Internal failure cost	Description
Knowledge loss	Costs due to delays while employees seek information that others have but which is not shared or available
Technology loss	Costs due to additional labor expenses due to IT controls and the complexity of limited access to required information
Discontinuity loss	Costs associated with workarounds and delays when employees have to respond to situations that are unexpected or that they are not trained for

These three types of losses can be a challenge to identify and are difficult to financially evaluate; they also may form part of the costs of aspects such as excess turnover. It is less important where they are reported than to ensure that the impact of such events is recognized.

Many organizations attempt to protect their intellectual capital through confidentiality agreements and other legal methods – and there may be legal costs that again form part of turnover. However, this is almost impossible to prove with tacit knowledge (which remains "in the head" of the employee) and it is hard to prove even with explicit knowledge that has been internally codified. A real loss occurs when tacit plus implicit knowledge is lost (i.e., both the knowledge in the employee's head and their experience of applying it within the organization).

The final segment might be considered a list of the possible other areas where costs are incurred that might be avoided or reduced if there was a higher level of communication, cooperation, collaboration, and commitment within the organization. A positive culture is one that enables and enhances the performance of the individual parts of a business model when they are working together effectively. While the parts (resources) have a financial cost (funding), the outcome is the result of the whole system; thus, what is being sought is excess funding of resources to reduce the system's output.

Internal failure cost	Description
Rework / repair	Costs associated with repeating work which was incomplete / sub-standard due to poor training, lack of knowledge or low motivation (occurs in all departments and activities); repeated paperwork processing; repeated IT support; IT problem fixes due to operator errors
Capability shortfall	Unplanned costs incurred over and above estimates due to a failure to evaluate capability when agreeing to customer contract (lack of knowledge, time or driven by closing the deal without consideration for operational impact)
Material losses	Scrapped materials lost due to non-compliant work that cannot be repaired or resolved (net of cost recovery)
Damage	Excess costs caused by "failure to care" by employees – inadequate attention to transport of fragile goods, damage to property, higher wear and tear on vehicles and equipment (including failure of IT equipment)
Shrinkage	Loss of materials or supplies taken by employees for personal use
Excess supplier costs	Additional costs incurred due to suppliers meeting product specifications but failing to meet service and relationship standards (non-compliant paperwork requiring added activity etc.)
Supplier trust losses	Excess costs caused when issues can only be solved via legal / contractual discussions due to a lack of shared values and trust between parties

Internal failure cost	Description
Consulting losses	Costs incurred through use of independent third parties that are called in to identify and recommend improvements already known by employees
Disposition costs	Excess costs incurred when failures internally require "make safe" and other actions prior to or during disposal
Excess call center costs	Excessive costs / activity in call centers due to poorly trained or motivated sales staff not providing accurate information to users
Sales productivity losses	Excessive sales time (and/or others) committed to resolution of customer problem caused by other staff – e.g., aggressively following up on overdue accounts when the error is company based, resulting in higher sales cost per unit of revenue
Equipment downtime / failure	All costs associated with failure of equipment where it is due to a "fix after failure" attitude, as well as where employee neglect / damage is involved; also due to lack of trust – employees are not allowed to either raise issues prior to failure, or take action to prevent and/or fix problems

Using one example from the above list related to call center costs, let's explore the impact further. Call centers are, by definition, support activities that respond to failures somewhere in the system. Many organizations see the costs of call centers as an overhead to be minimized; yet they are a window of opportunity for identifying "fixes to the system". Often, because of poor collaboration or the efforts to limit costs by "getting the client off the line" (poor culture), organizations miss the opportunity to identify the root cause of a problem and implement a fix, which would eliminate such calls altogether.

These examples are generic in nature and every organization operates its own unique business model. Therefore, while only some examples may be relevant, the best way to understand failures is to engage those involved in the processes and ask them to help identify wastage.

Failure costs – internal, summary
• Internal failure costs occur when a failure of desired behavior results in additional resources being spent.
• Most internal failure costs incurred are invisible because they are bundled with other labor (and their) expenses.
• Traditional accounting does not report causal drivers of the unplanned consumption of resources.
• While many failure costs are buried in labor costs, there will be third-party and other costs involved.
• Many events that drive excess costs may already be reported elsewhere (e.g., absenteeism) but the financial impact is rarely added.
• Many internal failure costs may be systemic (e.g., a narrower span of control due to less delegation and lower trust).
• Some failures will be easier to cost than others (e.g., loss of knowledge caused by [excess] turnover).
• Identification of failures is the most important action; classification (internal or external) and accuracy of costing are secondary to knowing the events and approximate costs.
• Poor culture can lead to systemic failures (e.g., fix after failure of equipment problems) where employees are disengaged, resulting in greater costs and downtime.
• Employees often know where these events are occurring.
Checklist
• Is there existing reporting of internal failure costs?
• Is there awareness of the breadth of potential excess costs due to behavioral issues?
• Is HR already using metrics that suggest a financial impact?
• How aware is your organization of events that are occurring internally as a result of poor culture?

The Cost of Poor Culture

8 Failure costs – external

> **Costs of poor culture – External failure costs**
> External failure costs result from behavior not conforming to expectations and requirements that are visible outside the organization, and that directly or indirectly affect stakeholders, such as customers, suppliers and other third parties.

External failure costs are made up of excess and unnecessary spending that is due to a negative culture; this impacts the organization externally, including impacts on suppliers and customers, clients, and brand value. External failure costs are visible outside the organization through their impact on key stakeholders, such as suppliers, customers, and clients, as well as the community, regulators and other third parties.

External failure costs might already be identified as specific expenses but many of them are again buried within other areas of operating costs and drive up the aggregate cost of doing business. In other words, management knows costs are too high, but the lack of visibility makes it difficult to address and eliminate the cost drivers.

Some key areas of external failure are already identifiable, yet many organizations do not track these or link them back to drivers related to behavior. The best example is **brand and reputation** that is tracked by organizations such as Brand Finance or Interbrand and published annually.

External failure cost	Description
Brand value loss	Reduction in brand value because of one or more activities in the marketplace
Reputation loss	Loss or decline of reputation in the market, affecting brand, investor attraction, etc.
Rebates and credits	Loss of revenues due to giving rebates or credits, or replacing services free of charge, as a result of poor employee interaction with client (attitude, training, time availability, etc.)
Investigation costs	Excess costs due to the time required to investigate problems and issues to determine the root causes, their resolution, and corrective action
Revenue losses	Loss of revenue (especially in service businesses) where clients fail to re-buy or renew contracts due to poor staff attitudes or lack of support (poor commitment, training, motivation, guidance, etc.); would also include the impact of losing market share due to relationship rather than product issues
Recall / market fix costs	Excess costs caused when product or service is pushed to market without full internal sign-off (often to meet sales quotas or quarterly results) and the product fails in the marketplace and must be fixed or re-called
Warranty costs	Similar to Recall costs; and includes costs under contractual commitments for a period of time after purchase
Market damage control	Additional costs incurred when the organization fails to adequately assess the risk of product impact in the market and is subsequently impacted by negative consequences from its use or application (poor risk management, priority on quarterly financials, specialist staff opinions ignored, etc.)

Organizations often take corrective action to resolve events caused by poor staff interaction. Externally, this can impact suppliers, customers, distributors, agents, regulators, and sub-contractors and even business partners. Such events are often indicators of underlying systemic problems related to culture – and may well be signs of the "moments of truth" discussed earlier. The focus should not stop at fixing the problem; these questions should continue to be asked: What caused this problem? and how can this be avoided in the future?

External failure cost	Description
Penalty costs	Costs imposed on the organization by clients and users under contractual commitment who failed to meet service standards
Fines and penalties	Excess costs incurred through fines and penalties imposed by third parties due to failures of compliance or assessed conduct / ethical problems
Cooperative losses	Additional costs incurred when suppliers and others fail to "go the extra mile" to resolve issues rapidly
Legal costs	Costs associated with defending action initiated by clients when support fails to meet standards and/or requirements, or where erroneous claims on capability are made by staff (untrained, driven by quota, etc.); could also include additional costs working with regulatory bodies
Promotional repair costs	Additional costs incurred to repair brand image when unplanned events have occurred that negatively impacted brand and reputation; could include costs associated with "damage control"
Premium interest costs	Negative impact on fees and interest costs where an organization is seen as an "ethical risk" by lenders due to poor behavior track record

External failure cost	Description
Talent loss	Where an organization's reputation is seen as negative, the ability to attract and retain "talent" will become a challenge requiring additional costs and potentially premium pay; typically, this will be an extra cost but also a temporary fix
Supplier damage control	Additional costs incurred when poor supplier selection and/or management results in activity that negatively impacts the buyer and requires either change of supplier and/or damage control

Once again, examples listed are generic, and some may be considered to belong in another category, such as talent loss (where the organization becomes less attractive to talent seeking work, so they decide to apply elsewhere). Again, the importance is in recognizing that the events are taking place and attempting to assess the impact on organizational resources, especially cost.

One major cost of failure - especially related to external failures even though it happens internally, is the "cost of escalation." It often happens that individuals within the organization fail to cooperate and collaborate and the result is that problems that need to be dealt with are unsolved; as a result, supervisors and managers become involved which can take up a significant part of their time. One example occurred in a large federal government department, where, because of staffing issues, a large number of employees were "acting" in temporary positions. Under the union agreement, every one of these people qualified to have their pay adjusted up to the level of the acting position they were temporarily involved in. Because of process problems the backlog of these pay adjustments had grown to such a level that employees pay was not adjusted until weeks after they completed their temporary assignment.

This problem resulted in employees asking their manager what the position was on their acting pay adjustment; the manager then spent time following up with HR to find what was happening and HR taking time to track the problem don and report. The analysis that my organization conducted demonstrated that the financial impact of the time and effort spent on this amounted to over $7 million annually. Our recommendation was that the company invest in actions necessary to reduce the backlog as well as resolve the staffing problem as we were certain that an amount less than $7 million would bring a significant payback (as well as having positive impact on moral of both managers and staff). This was a clear "cost of failure" (although in this case an internal failure"

An example of an external failure was experienced by a manufacturer who was building major electrical switchgear. One export customer was having problems but there were inadequate technical support resources (budgetary constraints). This resulted in multiple overseas trips to solve the problem at the customers location by an increasingly level of experienced person, that was only ended when it was realized that the service cost had exceeded the cost of replacing the product completely.

No organization can afford hidden and unplanned excess costs but the level of understanding of how people are using their time is often not well understood. This is especially true of those in management positions. As business has become more competitive and complex, managers need to devote as much time as possible to their roles of planning, monitoring and leading. Yet many face significant demands of their time to address issues and problems that have been escalated by others in the organization. This hidden cost and its impact on an organization's health is significant but unreported (and can lead to management stress and burn out as well as other internal and personal issues).

In these times of attention being paid to the societal impact of organizational behavior, external failure costs become even more important, especially as "externalities." These should be considered both as a driver and as an impact for organizations that have adopted ESG reporting and who may have looked at the UN SDGs at the strategy level (see Chapter 2). The list shows some of the most significant of these.

External failure cost	Description
Public health care impact	Costs borne by community / taxpayer due to workplace accidents
Mental health costs	Costs incurred internally and externally relative to employees (and others) suffering from workplace induced challenges
Environmental fines and penalty	Costs incurred externally due to employee actions resulting in unplanned emissions and discharges
Tax impact	Cost to the community of the organization minimizing local taxation through global tax planning (difference between local notional tax and actual amounts paid)

These last types of failures are controversial and start addressing the "ethically correct" conduct of an organization versus its "compliance with the law." This is a rapidly changing dynamic for organizations to consider as social change occurs and expectations change. The reporting of the costs of a poor culture are important, but equally important, especially in the developing area of integrated reporting, would be the expenditures required to establish and maintain a good culture.

Areas of prevention and appraisal costs offer the opportunity to identify these types of expenditure as they contribute to sustaining a positive culture, which reflects specifically on the investments required to sustain a social "license to operate," as well as to deliver "non-financial" value to stakeholders other than investors – although investors will realize at some point that a positive culture lowers the risk of poor conduct and also sustains market value of their investment.

Failure costs – external, summary
• External failure costs are incurred when unplanned events have financial implications and are visible externally.
• Behavioral issues can have significant financial impacts due to regulation of compliance failures.
• Such failures can result in fines, penalties, and unplanned fees and expenses (including legal).
• External failures can occur in areas of the supply chain when poor or ineffective communications, collaboration, and other interactions cause problems.
• External failures often occur due to poor interactions between the organization and its clients or customers.
• External failures can cause a higher client churn rate, creating a systemic increase in sales and marketing costs.
• External failures can also be caused by negative interactions between employees and other third parties.
• External failures can have significant financial implications on brand value and organizational reputation.
• External failures can become an "externality" and be passed on to a non-related party such as community or society. This can have an impact on "social license."
• Reputation loss can also affect "employer attractiveness," resulting in higher hiring costs as well as loss of ability to attract scarce talent.

Checklist
• How complex is the business model in terms of relationships with external organizations?
• Are there key external relationships where interactions are critical to strategic and operational success?
• Is the breadth of potential external failures recognized?
• Does the organization understand the link between expectations of behavior externally and their brand and reputation?

9 Failure costs – strategic

> ***Cost of poor culture – Strategic failure costs***
> Strategic failure costs are typically the financial impacts from lost opportunities that occur because of attitudes or actions that reduce organizational growth, creativity, and innovation.

The impact of strategic failure comes from lost opportunities to enhance competitive advantage caused by poor culture, including impacts from lost input and ideas from employees, customers, clients, community, and others. The challenge for many organizations – and especially from accounting – is that these are not real costs but missed opportunities, therefore they cannot be included as "ongoing costs of poor culture." However, they are strategically critical; where poor culture holds back innovation, creativity and improvement, changes that could be made to further reduce costs and improve products and services in the marketplace will be lost.

There may be some ability to calculate an implicit level of these costs through competitive benchmarking. If an organization can develop comparative innovation rates, improvement rates, growth rates or quality levels of competitors that they seem unable to achieve, and if it is already felt that what is holding things back is either poor employee relations or other issues related to poor culture, then the financial impact of these gaps can be developed as lost strategic opportunity. This can even be done at the process level where processes do not seem to be as effective as those of competitors. One key sign that a problem may exist is where an organization is constantly under cost pressures and seeks to resolve profitability issues by reducing staff; this often perpetuates the challenge, as the remaining staff are further demotivated and are often under greater pressure to perform. This, in turn, leads to higher absenteeism and potential health problems. Loss of key staff – even those who may be paid at the top-of-market rates – is another sign that the problem is not money but culture.

More than 25 years ago, when many organizations were facing cost challenges and were resorting to significant downsizing, the byline of the book, *Grow to be Great: Breaking the Downsizing Cycle*[24] was "no company ever shrank to greatness." The book contained a diagnostic "thinking map," the first two questions of which were:

- Are you growing relative to the industry and competitors (revenue and profit)?
- What is your cost position relative to your competitors?

This was long before people were talking about corporate culture, yet there is parallel to "people engagement" in the alternative actions suggested in the replies to those two questions:

- Consider pruning or fixing unprofitable segments.
- Consider the possibilities for reinventing the entire business.
- (Undertake a) Customer Value diagnostic.
- (Undertake an) Economics diagnostic.
- (Undertake an) Execution diagnostic.

---

[24] Gertz, D.L. and Baptista, J. P. A., 1995. *Grow to be Great: Breaking the Downsizing Cycle*, Free Press.

For each of these suggested activities, a workforce that was fully engaged, and had great relationships with suppliers, customers, and others, would likely already have suggested improvements in all these areas. A diagnostic would not be necessary – your people would already have acted.

Leading organizations such as Toyota face the same pressures and realities as many of their competitors in terms of advances in technology and economic change. However, over the years, organizations wishing to emulate the success of such leaders, have looked for elements of their management approach to follow. One of these has been the Japanese concept of "Kaizen," or continuous improvement: a gradual and methodical process that is based on applying the "Five S" system:

Seiri	Sort	*Seiri* is based on the premise that employees are distracted by unnecessary objects in the workspace, reducing their productivity
Seition	Set in order	*Seition* is the process of placing objects in the right place for action
Seiso	Shine	*Seiso* is based on the notion that a clean workplace is safer, has less distractions, and is more rigorously maintained
Seiketsu	Standardize	*Seiketsu* requires the establishment of standards that help ensure that whatever improvements are made using Kaizen or the 5S approach to continuous improvement become the norm
Shitsuke	Sustain	*Shitsuke* is the process by which new processes are adopted and encouraged to become habitual

The basic definition of continuous improvement lies in the thinking and leadership approach used. The constant attention to opportunities must be part of organizational culture – and this only happens when the environment in the workplace encourages employee engagement and places people in leadership positions are actively engaged in developing a human-centric approach. One can see that involvement and engagement, especially allowing employees a high level of input to their workspace, is foundational to developing a continual improvement mindset.

The following list identifies the types of lost opportunity that exist when an organization operates with a poor, or "non-optimum," culture; these first items demonstrate the mindset needed in approach to everyday work, as well as opportunities for improvement:

Strategic failure cost	Description
Limited continual improvement	Operational costs are not being continually reduced, causing margin shrinkage and resulting in programs for cost reduction that often fail to remove the root cause of excess costs, leading to lowering of morale; the organization struggles to sustain a competitive advantage
Limited innovation	Related to the above; lip service is paid to new ideas from employees; feedback is slow or non-existent and managers / leaders do not actively encourage employee innovation; the result is a maturing of capability and offerings which can often only be resolved through mergers / acquisitions or the "buying in" of patents and product / service opportunities
Limited ability to benefit from being "lean"	A lean organization is, by definition, one where there are extremely low levels of waste; however, to be "lean" requires cooperation and collaboration across traditional functional organizational silos and a willingness of employees to take on more caring and responsibility; where people feel they are valued and recognized, lean initiatives will probably bring greater positive results

Clearly, these lost opportunities can only be manifested by total system performance. The underlying causes are certainly not clearly illustrated by any financial reporting, so the main measure is lower-than-desired profitability; the response to this – due to lack of knowledge about the root cause – is across-the-board cost reductions. The next list of strategic failure costs reflects failures to heed external signs or opportunities that indicate change is needed:

Strategic failure cost	Description
Responsiveness (market)	Organizations today seek to be agile and responsive, qualities that come from employees who care and are willing to collaborate, cooperate, and communicate; in short, they are fully committed through what they do to the success of the business, and a positive culture is one that creates the right atmosphere so that, if these human qualities are not present, the organization will not attain the capability
Responsive (change)	Organizations need to be able to respond rapidly to changing markets and deploy their changes as rapidly as possible; effective leadership, which fully embraces its human capital and creates a culture of trust and commitment, will develop a foundation for rapid deployment of change
Responsive (regulatory)	For many organizations, the regulatory framework within which they operate holds the power to support (speed up) or frustrate (slow down) certain business initiatives and changes; open and transparent communications with regulators and a trust in its commitment to behavior, compliance and responsiveness will likely result in better support and trust from regulators when required

The final items reflect the impact that a disengaged workforce eventually has on an organization's reputation, especially when it is seeking to attract new people with key skills that may be in demand. Informal "reputational" social media sites, such as Glassdoor, collect and make available information about employers globally.

Strategic failure cost	Description
Reputation loss	While purchase decisions are heavily financially based, increasingly products are not differentiated, and the "ability to do business" with the company – i.e., the interactions between staff and clients, becomes a key competitive edge, so a positive reputation through staff who are knowledgeable, and care becomes an asset in retaining clients and growing sales
Talent attraction	In many knowledge-based companies, attraction and retention of human talent is a core requirement; creating a reputation generated by existing employees as "a great place to work" will enhance the attraction of potential talent (especially in a competitive market where people have choices) as well as reduce hiring costs
Investor attraction	Investors are becoming increasingly concerned with organizational behavior, in particular as it relates to the risk of their investment (both capital and returns); organizations that develop, sustain, and communicate positive attributes that are seen to reduce risk will have less challenge attracting investors and will possibly pay a smaller financial risk premium on borrowing

Investor attraction can also become an important strategic issue; the "cost of money" is one of many costs of doing business and is usually related to both cost of fixed-term money (such as loan interest) and expectations for profitability, both of which are related to an investor's assessment of risk. The marketplace is not yet mature enough to fully understand the impact of culture on both profitability and the potential related to "enterprise sustainability." However, there are signs of this changing, particularly where related to investor interest in ESG reporting, although currently the main focus remains on climate change. The "S" and "G" of ESG have not yet matured to a level of meaningful reporting relative to culture risk.

Failure costs – strategic, summary
• Strategic failure costs are systemic and lead to competitive disadvantage.
• Systemic failure of continual improvement is a core aspect of the risk from strategic failure.
• Poor culture leads to lack of innovation, creativity, responsiveness, commitment, and lean thinking.
• Strategic failure costs tend to show up in a decline in competitiveness over time.
• Benchmarking can help provide insight into gradual declines in systemic competitiveness.
• A bias towards cost containment through downsizing is an indicator of creeping strategic failure in culture.
• Lower levels of responsiveness to market, regulatory, and other changes indicate systemic failure of culture.
• The level of workforce resistance to change and the time to execute change are indicators of the strategic health of culture.

Checklist
• Is there a lethargy towards change demonstrated by the workforce?
• Is cost containment a constant battle, addressed mainly through forced downsizing?
• Is the organization faced by increased competitive pressures relative to competitors in revenue, quality, output, or cost?

10 Developing an action plan

The approach to understanding the impact of the costs of a poor culture (COPC) should be a journey from simplicity to more in-depth under-standing; each stage will require a higher level of analytical thinking and, ultimately, be included in business planning and strategic thinking. Each step will be a learning process and will generally follow Crosby's five "stages of maturity" that were explained in Chapter 3.

Readers should not be distracted by assuming that the actual buried costs at Stage 1, Uncertainty, are actually 20%. Most organizations are ignorant of the impact of poor culture. However, it is known that, in using systems thinking, the under-utilized capability of a system of integrated resources can often hide at least this level of opportunity. The important challenge is that a small change in people's performance can be magnified both in terms of bottom-line impact and in revenue growth.

There are four steps in developing an understanding of the cost of poor culture and assessing the financial impact, that will be covered in the next four sections:

- Get leadership on board and educate those involved in initial activity.
- Use what data – both financial and non-financial – might already be available.
- Develop areas to investigate using employee involvement through brainstorming approaches.

- Start reporting some examples of the financial impact of poor culture, review, and repeat.

While consultants might be used to provide education and training, for facilitation, and for the initial assessment of areas to investigate, it is important that the approach is led internally. This should start with a small group of people, ideally from a variety of backgrounds and functions, who already have an interest in this subject and a belief that opportunity for improvement exists. It is important to involve both HR and accounting functions; however, others might be added. It is also critical that a sponsoring executive at the "C" suite level is responsible for the initial project.

10.1 Develop awareness – leadership, education, and training.

As in any change initiative, people need to understand what's going on; therefore, selecting a champion to lead the efforts, who has a strong operational bias as well as an understanding of how processes and activities drive costs, will be important. This individual should gather a team of like-minded "change agents" from different departments to act as a steering group. This team should then map out a plan as how to proceed, starting with clear communication, explaining what the initiative to understand the costs of poor culture is all about.

The initial stage of building awareness has several important goals to achieve that underpin the potential for success:

- Senior management must be supportive – not only in words but also by being engaged in the activity.
- A "C-suite" executive should act as champion of the initiative, or it is unlikely to carry weight at the "C-suite" level.
- Focus on a manageable work area as a pilot approach.
- Use examples and case studies or articles wherever possible to support the potential for performance improvements.

Once there is senior-level support, a project leader and team, and an initial understanding of what types of cost are being looked for, the pilot should begin.

10.2 Look for what is already available.

Using the guidance in this document, the team should work with finance – in particular, those involved with an understanding of operating costs, such as management accountants, or Financial Plans and Analysis if this exists. This group should review the concepts of COPC and look for existing cost information (typically line items for expenses within the existing financial records – the GL) that can clearly be linked to one or more of the main cost categories. While the focus should be on events that would be considered "waste," i.e., failures, other categories such as prevention could also be captured.

While some costs may already be expressed in financial terms in the accounting records, many will be buried within other cost categories – in particular, payroll costs. The team should look for non-financial data that is currently available and start by understanding the events that are taking place; once these are available, the team can work with finance and start answering the question: What is this event costing us every time it happens? Then they can identify where the costs are currently being reported. Human resources metrics will be extremely valuable as a starting point; in many cases HR is already reporting its own metrics, yet the costs of these events have never been reported on a regular basis. Although each organization will be different, some starting ideas are:

Existing financial data
- Regulatory penalties and fines
- Safety / safe working penalties and fines
- Agency labor costs (cover for vacancies)
- Credits and settlements with customers for problems
- Penalties paid to suppliers for relationship problems.
- Damages, shortages, and other waste

- Legal costs related to HR / employee disputes.
- Unplanned termination costs

Existing HR data
- Absentee, sickness (costed to show labor + other costs)
- Turnover (costed to show cost of hiring + orientation and other training)
- Candidate failure rate (costed to reflect cost of interviews with operational staff)
- Escalation costs (time taken for staff to investigate and attend meetings, board, committees, etc.)
- Acting pay (premium amounts being paid to acting roles under union agreements as no staff available)

If there is an adequate base of information to start reporting, then these costs should be collected and reported on a regular basis as the initial step in demonstrating the impact of COPC. The goal is to create the basis for a dialogue on what is happening and why, and investigate what can be done to improve things, rather than to assign blame or responsibility.

There may be a natural bias to assume that many failure costs are incurred by HR responding to the impact of culture problems; however, "people issues" can impact across an organization. Time is taken by non-HR staff, such as supervisors and managers, maintenance staff, legal staff, accounting, and many others. Thus, the COPC permeates the whole structure, resulting in operating costs that are higher than needed. This is where the next part of the action plan is used to generate ideas about where the problems and issues are hidden.

10.3 Brainstorm events that are caused by poor culture.
This stage will involve members of the team brainstorming with other employees to ask the question: What do we do around here that we would not need to spend time doing if everyone cooperated and collaborated effectively? The events and processes that are identified may happen occasionally, while some may be more frequent or even worse, are seen

and accepted as "the way things are" – a clear indication of hidden problems. At this stage, it does not matter if no one knows what costs are incurred for such events, because this can be calculated later. For now, the aim is identification of such events.

Poor culture often results in employees and others not making suggestions for improvement because no one seems to be listening; and even when someone does listen, nothing seems to change. This is their opportunity to think about their day-to-day work and identify what gets in the way of them being productive. From the list of events, the team can first select those that are easy to identify and track. The list can then be reviewed for factors that will determine which ones to start collecting information on and reporting, including:

- Do we already track the event?
- If not, how easy would it be to start collecting information?
- How often does this event occur?
- Are the steps / activities that occur to fix the problem similar each time, or are there different levels of seriousness or complexity?
- Would it be straightforward to estimate costs incurred for the event?
- If we collect the data, how simple or complex might the task of fixing the problem be?

Based on the results of these questions, a rating approach can be used to score the various events with the goal of collecting data – maybe on the top five if there are many. The event that can be reported fastest can be used for a pilot program; events can be dropped, or new ones added, depending upon how valuable the information seems to be after a few periods of reporting.

Financial support can be enlisted to develop costs associated with COPC events as they occur; typically, the costs are already included somewhere in the financials, but are buried within expenses like labor, outside services, or other single-line items.

Typical events

- Supervisor spending time to resolve inter-departmental disputes and issues.
- Supervisory costs associated with HR systems issues (e.g., payment problems, pay disputes, benefit problems, vacation problems)
- HR time spent on resolving supervisor / employee disputes, especially attitude, treatment, etc.
- IT (or other) support costs incurred due to equipment damage by employees.
- Escalation meeting for grievances or disputes
- Waiting for instructions or information
- Researching information that is already known and available.
- Putting things in writing to protect yourself (CYA)

The pilot team, together with those who have identified the selected COPC events, can set up an informal reporting process to track when the event occurs. They can then apply costs to each occurrence to come up with an event-based cost of failure; it is important not to worry about accuracy at this stage (70% plus is a good guide). The costs can then be summarized and included in the report, adding them to existing events listed in the first (what is already available) stage.

10.4 Evaluate results, act, and repeat.

The goal at this stage is to develop increased awareness in the organization of how the current approach to collaboration, cooperation, communications, and other areas – "how we do things around here" – is increasing costs that are hidden. The team can then use this information to work with all levels of employees to ask the question: What do we need to do differently? From the responses to this, an action plan should begin to take shape, through which gradual changes and improvements can be seen.

Getting an understanding of the failure costs related to a poor culture will be a trial-and-error process; some items being reported may turn out to be unimportant and can be dropped, while others might need to be added. Continual learning and improvement are key at this stage. Results should be capable of being tracked as the occurrence of negative events starts to decrease, resulting in lower costs. The single largest problem will be a management / leadership attitude that looks for blame and immediate improvement as this pilot process moves forward. Such an approach will destroy whatever trust might have existed or had started to be built. Unless the "C-suite" is solidly behind this initiative and wants to create real change in the way the organization operates, there is no point starting. Culture is about attitude, and it starts at the top.

10.5 The need for revolution
A key challenge for many organizations may be created through the realization that there is a significant problem and financial impact from an existing poor culture. This can have "political" implications, with certain people being opposed to critical changes taking place.

Cultural change can sometimes only be achieved through a significant event – evolution and continual improvement may initially not be enough. This is the reason why senior management must be supportive of the initiative and must be prepared to accept the needs for change, even at leadership levels. For example, the first key change might involve retirement, re-organization, or other significant changes in leadership.

10.6 Heading down the wrong path
Management has always been concerned about low productivity and will seek advice on how performance can be improved. A high percentage of published literature on the subject suggests that areas like social media are the underlying causes of poor productivity and that employees should not be allowed to access these on personal devices at work (even though many already work using the internet and various hand-held devices). Many may

suggest stronger policies and discipline to avoid gossiping and extended coffee breaks.

Most of these ideas and policies are misguided and, in most cases, will lower employee morale (further). It might be interesting to reflect that many years ago the availability of (land line) phones in offices were restricted because it was assumed that people would waste time using them for personal reasons. Similarly, when copying machines were introduced, it was thought use of them had to be controlled because staff would be making personal-use copies.

However, in general, staff waste time because they are not engaged in the work that they are employed to do. If organizations select the right people, treat them well, and build an environment of trust, respect, collaboration, and cooperation, then the problem of people spending time on non-work activities will almost disappear. Should it happen, either peer pressure or a focused approach with the individual might be necessary. The solution of putting policies and procedures in place that control the actions of all of the employees because a few are unaware or unwilling to commit to the organization is not the right answer.

Creating an effective culture starts as a governance issue and takes time to permeate every aspect of an organization's activity. There are no quick fixes and the desire to fix it fast will likely backfire. People leadership is a core talent for managers in the 21st century but even those who embrace a people-centric approach will fail if the whole organization is not fully committed.

10.7 Summary

There is a cost associated with poor culture and a lack of cooperation, communications, and collaboration. The existence of functional isolation, the building of corporate silos and "protecting turf" are at the heart of slow down activities, often causing increased expenditures and duplication of work.

Understanding how culture impacts the financial competitiveness of an organization is a critical piece of strategic knowledge that must be developed so that organizations can remove constraints and optimize costs. This structured approach to understanding both the problem areas (failures) and the investments necessary to protect against failures brings together information that may already exist but for which the total organizational impact is not realized.

Developing an action plan, summary
• There are four levels of awareness of the financial impact of a poor culture.
• Belief in the hidden opportunity for improvement must drive a strategic change initiative.
• Senior leadership must own and be engaged in the initiative to identify the cost of poor culture.
• Existing data, both financial and non-financial, will form the basis of a starting point for reporting costs.
• Non-financial event data can be utilized to start evaluating buried costs.
• All initiatives must start with education and training.
• A pilot approach in one area can provide a great learning process.
• Start reporting the "low hanging fruit" – items that can be easily collected, and action taken to fix.
• Be prepared to iterate – experiment. Try collecting items and if they are not important, move on.
• Expand the pilot and add to them team – educate, train, implement, learn, repeat.
• Avoid knee-jerk reactions to waste – social media use, coffee talk, gossip, etc.; aim for the root cause of disengagement.
• Hang in there – keep going, as it will take time to see the benefits, but attitudes will start changing.

Checklist
• Have you developed / obtained materials to educate / convince senior management to support the effort?
• Has a senior "C-suite" executive been appointed with accountability for the project?
• Has an initial, cross-functional team been established who are committed to the development of a cost of poor culture initiative?
• Is there data than can be used to start the process – either financial or non-financial?
• Can a brainstorming session be run in one or two select areas to start the initiative?
• Has the brainstorming developed a "big list" of possible events that can be investigated?
• Has the list been ranked based on criteria to aid some early wins?

The Cost of Poor Culture

11 Bridging to ISO 30414

In 2018, the International Standards Organization published ISO 30414 *Human resource management — Guidelines for internal and external human capital reporting*; this document was developed by TC (Technical Committee) # 260 that is working on Human Capital Management standards, guidelines, and technical specifications. These documents have increased in importance as the implementation of integrated reporting has also progressed; recent requirements for human capital reporting by the SEC has further encouraged the use of HR metrics.

The key challenge is that many of the metrics provide little insight into the financial risk and implications for an organization; until metrics are seen as organizational measures and not silo-based, functional measures, this will continue. Understanding the cost of a poor culture begins to provide the opportunity for financial and HR collaboration.

ISO 30414 provides a list of about 60 metrics under 11 categories that cover key aspects of HR management:

- Compliance and ethics
- Costs
- Diversity
- Leadership
- Organizational culture
- Organizational health, safety, and well-being
- Productivity

- Recruitment, mobility, and turnover
- Skills and capabilities
- Succession planning
- Workforce availability

These categories as well as the whole document will probably be revised and updated in the years to come but they provide a good starting point.

Some suggested ISO metrics might support financial information for prevention costs to provide some insight into the level of investment being made to prevent culture failures. Examples of these are:

- % Of employees who have completed training on compliance and ethics.
- Leadership development.
- % Of employees who participate in training.
- Total training costs.

It is beyond this book to discuss the quality and composition of the metrics being proposed by ISO; however, it does demonstrate the potential for collaboration to produce more meaningful information.

Failure costs might be a bit more interesting as many HR metrics are already in use for reporting, but it is rare to see these expressed in "real" financial terms. Accounting currently does a poor job of explaining where the money goes when it comes to why spending occurs; this is especially true when it relates to money being spent – buried in operating expenses, related to HR corrective action – i.e., the impact of a poor culture.

As an example, an organization can incur certain costs due to poor culture that show up as HR metrics. Some examples of HR reporting metrics from ISO 30414 are:

- number and type of grievances filed.

- number and types of disciplinary actions.
- disputes referred to third parties.
- costs per hire.
- recruitment costs.
- turnover costs (and turnover rate).
- span of control.
- lost time to injuries.
- number of occupational accidents.
- number of people killed at work.
- average time to fill critical vacancies.
- percentage of positions filled internally.
- successor coverage rate.
- absenteeism.

Every one of the above HR metrics has financial implications that impact operating costs. If, for example costs per hire and turnover rate were combined it would give a financial picture of the level of expenses being incurred. This rate could then be compared to either a strategic goal related to turnover, or an industry or other benchmark, and the difference between the actual and the benchmark reported as an excess cost (or cost saving).

In the case of accidents (or death) there might be zero tolerance from a governance perspective – but adding financial costs to the HR statistic would provide a deeper understanding of the impact on the financial stakeholder. Extending these costs to provide information on the externalities would begin to demonstrate the impact of work-related problems on wider society. This might include taxpayers where health care is government funded, or the insurance company that is paying out on the claims.

Span of control, which drives the level of supervisory positions, may be higher than it could be because of lack of trust and delegation (or even skills and competencies) in the workforce. There are costs to the existing structure which could be reduced if the levels of trust and delegation could be improved. There are also costs associated with the COPC appraisal activities. Additional levels of approval and decision making will slow down innovation and creativity and add expenses to the organization.

One key area that is often overlooked is the challenge of internal controls: often span of control, as well as approval levels and delegation of authority, are established as key aspects of internal control following risk assessment. A more streamlined organization could be implemented if more checks were performed at the time of hiring to assess the probability of undesired behavior. More investment in leadership development could build a higher degree of trust and allow greater authority to be passed down in the organizational structure.

Even if financial aspects have been developed as part of HR metrics, e.g., as cost of hire, these can be incomplete and not reflect the full cost to the organization. For example, cost of hire should include two core aspects: the actual hiring process and expenses for preparing the person to be "work-ready." One is an acquisition cost, the other an investment. The real cost of hiring, and the number that should be used as a failure cost when losses are higher than expected, must reflect the *total* resources incurred.

The following information on the first aspect – the actual cost of hiring – is similar to that suggested by ISO, where the cost of hiring is determined as all external and internal costs incurred for hiring during a year (or equivalent period), divided by the number of people hired during that period:

- **External hiring costs** comprise all sources of spending outside the organization on recruiting efforts during the period in question. Examples include third-party agency fees, advertising costs, job fair costs, expenses for assessments, and travel costs during the recruiting effort.

- **Internal hiring costs** include all internal resources and costs used for staffing efforts during the period in question. Examples include the fully loaded salary and benefits of the recruiting team, and fixed costs such as physical infrastructure (talent acquisition system costs, etc.).
- The **total number of hires** is the number of hires made in the evaluation period, regardless of the staffing type (regular full-time, regular part-time, etc.). It is assumed that whatever the total number of hires is, the fully loaded costs for the efforts taken to staff the positions are calculated in external and internal costs.

There are several problems with these definitions. First, hiring is not generic in nature and, where possible, different types should be separated. As a minimum, one would expect costs per hire to be broken down between "key position" staff, which would, by definition, take longer, other full-time permanent staff, temporary staff, and part-time staff. The processes for hiring may be different depending upon who is being hired, e.g., using an agency for temporary or part-time staff.

There are also significant support costs associated with certain hiring, such as time spent by non-HR people in developing or confirming job requirements, raising requisitions, working with HR on the requirements and then participating in interviews.

The second aspect – of work readiness – that should be considered as a cost of hire would include all mandatory training, such as health and safety, ethics or values training, and other requirements that must be completed before the person is work-ready. It is the total cost of all these resources that represents the organization's investment in the hiring process. As can be seen, just following the "minimum standard" would understate the financial impact of hires.

If the "cost of hire" data were combined with a target retention or turnover statistic, the organizational impact – of either positive or negative performance – on the goals would be seen. As financial reporting currently reveals, all these costs are buried as part of operating costs. Even if HR starts publishing cost of hire statistics, it only has impact when the resource effect on other stakeholders is seen.

The ISO 30414 framework for HR reporting metrics demonstrates the growing importance of comparable approaches across and between organizations, but this is at an early stage. While many reporting frameworks, such as the <IR> (Integrated Reporting developed by the IIRC) avoid prescriptive approaches, there are others, such as GRI, SASB, and IFAC, for example, who are trying to move toward standardization. While this might work for certain metrics that create value for some stakeholders, the organization itself needs to understand the concept of culture and to develop its own metrics before trying to force fit external standards.

Bridging to ISO 30414, summary
• ISO 30414 Guidelines for internal and external reporting provide some foundational HR metrics.
• There are 11 categories and about 60 individual metrics, most of which are non-financial.
• HR/human capital reporting is a growing area of investor and regulatory attention.
• The guidelines include some rudimentary financial data but information on performance impact is limited.
• Many of the metrics provided can be used as a foundation for events that can be financially developed.
• Metrics that are developed as part of cost of culture will find application as metrics under ISO 30414.
• Other bodies are developing standards for HR reporting but there is limited consensus.
Checklist
• Is the organization aware of the human resource management guidelines and other materials created by ISO TC 260?
• Has the organization reviewed the metrics within ISO 30414 and compared these to its own operation?
• Is there an opportunity to apply aspects of ISO 30414 to the development of a cost-of-culture framework?

The Cost of Poor Culture

114

12 Goodwill and impairment

In recent years, mergers, and acquisitions (M&A) have created a growing level of goodwill on the acquirer's balance sheets. This "accounting created value" occurs when the amount the buyer is willing to pay for an acquired organization exceeds its book value (the amount shown on the balance sheet) plus any adjustments allowed.

What the buyer is purchasing is a "system," the business model includes financial resources, including property, plant, and equipment (tangibles) together with intangibles or other assets. These other assets include people, customer relationships, supplier relationships, brand, reputation, knowledge, and other items that have been brought together to create products or services. The financial resources are essentially the book value. As the importance of people and other intangibles has increased, these have become a greater proportion of the amount the buyer is willing to pay; thus, goodwill has been increasing.

The overall price and the level of goodwill a buyer is willing to pay can be causally related to the effectiveness of an organization's culture. In these situations, the selling organization may have created a significant competitive advantage by building a positive culture that enables a high level of collaboration, cooperation, and commitment among key resources, and this may have created a system that is producing better than average performance. In this situation, the buyer faces a significant risk if this culture is changed or disrupted – which is often the case – as buyers attempt to integrate different organizations to achieve economies of scale.

One example of the types of changes that can occur is described in the *LA Times*[25]

> Immediately after the acquisition (in 2015), AT&T began making cuts in DirecTV's vaunted customer service operation, which ran centers in Idaho, Oklahoma, and Alabama. AT&T folded the group into its "shared services" division. Offshore call centers in the Philippines and India also were tasked with diagnosing satellite TV issues and fielding questions about other AT&T products. AT&T defended the move, saying centralization is an efficient way to support its plethora of products. But the change in ownership also led to a culture clash.

The article goes on to explain how in the DirectTV culture, people with ideas were encouraged to share and explore them and were supported, but since the acquisition, they are expected to stay in their place. It also explains how several DirectTV senior executives left with large payouts after the acquisition and a lot of knowledge about the business "walked out the door." (This problem seems to be continuing with AT&T appearing to seek to divest its media activities).

This is one of thousands of experiences with goodwill. While the acquiring organization is initially willing to pay the premium price for a successful system, making changes often starts to deplete and weaken the system and the underlying culture. The level of investors' funds paid for goodwill has been increasing. Duff & Phelps, in their annual report on goodwill trends in the USA for 2019[26], show that M&A of publicly traded companies generated *an additional goodwill amount of $391 billion that was added to corporate balance sheets, and a write-off for during for impairment during the year, of $71 billion."* Organizations must review their goodwill on an annual basis and determine whether it has been impaired. These impairment charges

---

[25] *LA Times*, January 31, 2020. "Nearly 3 million subscribers ditched DirecTV last year. Will AT&T do the same?" (Meg James).

[26] Duff & Phelps, 2020. US Impairment study for year ended December 2019.

might be felt as somewhat subjective once two organizations are integrated. However, the US accounting standards body, FASB, is concerned enough about the way the write-offs are being handled that they have made a review and update part of their 2021 work plan. The numbers are significant. The table below demonstrates that for many organizations goodwill, from acquisitions forms a large proportion of the organizations total declared financial assets. This list represents the top fifteen goodwill values of public companies in the US:

	Goodwill	Total assets	% of assets
Allergan	$45.9	$101.8	45.1%
Medtronic	$40.0	$89.7	44.6%
CVS Health	$78.7	$196.5	40.1%
United Health Group	$58.9	$152.2	38.7%
Procter & Gamble	$45.2	$118.3	38.2%
United Technologies	$48.1	$134.2	35.8%
Pfizer	$53.4	$159.4	33.5%
DuPont	$59.0	$188.0	31.4%
Cigna	$44.5	$153.2	29.0%
AT&T	$146.4	$531.9	27.5%
Comcast	$66.2	$251.7	26.3%
General Electric	$59.6	$309.1	19.3%
Berkshire Hathaway	$81.0	$707.8	11.4%
Bank of America	$69.0	$2,354.5	2.9%
JPMorgan Chase	$47.5	$2,622.5	1.8%
Top 15 Goodwill values	**$943.4**	**$8,070.8**	**11.7%**

These top fifteen companies are carrying about $1 trillion in goodwill, which is about 12% of the asset balances but a much higher percentage of their net book value after liabilities are deducted. As an example, AT&T's financial liabilities at this point were $338.0 billion, so the net book value was $193.9 of which goodwill was $146.4 or 76%. In other words, goodwill has become a substantial asset on corporate balance sheets.

These numbers are obviously significant and reflect the failure of accounting to provide a meaningful substantiation of what is being purchased, how it can be identified and through that, what steps might be necessary to avoid impairment. FASB, the US accounting standards board, has already provided guidance on the treatment of acquired intangibles in acquisition (Rule 142) but this provides only minimal solutions for the size of the problem.

It also demonstrates what might be considered the "shaky" financials of some organizations, where their book value without goodwill is even smaller, compared to market value. Business journals and papers have increasingly been reporting on the challenges this problem poses such as a 2020 article in the *Wall Street Journal*[27]

Goodwill used to be referred to as a "nothing" and many financial managers suggest that goodwill that is created from a merger should immediately be written off as a charge against equity (the owners accumulated "value"). This is an interesting approach as it would reflect the same accounting treatment that occurred when the initial investment in intangibles was made by the acquired company. It was written off against current earnings. However, this suggests that the practice of pretending intangibles have no role in assessing risk and management performance should continue, rather than attempting efforts to try and develop alternative approaches to understanding "where the money went" and whether the significant investments made to create these intangibles should, in some way be addressed. Either way, a large amount of shareholders funds is being assigned to developing business model capabilities, that are invisible.

Goodwill was created as a "quick fix" to keep the accounting records in balance. While the amount of goodwill was relatively small this remained a reasonably acceptable practice. Today, when organizations are directing an

---

[27] *Wall Street Journal*, January 21, 2020. "Goodwill Sparks Deep Division, at Least on Balance Sheets" (by John Eaglesham).

increasing number of resources into developing business models that contain the majority of "capabilities" as intangibles, the problem is far greater.

The focus on investing in corporate culture will hasten this challenge. As money flows into prevention costs, investments will be made that bring longer term benefits. These investments will reflect the building of the business model.

One only has to look at many organizations that are based on technology application to see the size of the issue. We have already discussed the major gap between market and book value of organizations like Amazon, Google (Alphabet), Facebook, Netflix, and Apple. But consider the amounts of money that venture capitalists and early investors have sunk into building business models into organizations that are more recent entrants such as Lyft, Uber, Snowflake and Doordash. All of these and many others that went public over the last few years have few tangible assets yet market values in the billions. Hidden problems can exist - as an example millions had already poured into Uber when there was a major cultural issue that caused its' valuation to drop by over $20 billion. As larger proportions of publicly traded organizations have intangible based business model, their stock market values are ticking time bombs!

Goodwill and impairment, summary
<ul><li>An aspect of goodwill reflects the monetization of investments made in creating an effective corporate culture.</li><li>Goodwill is created when a buyer purchases (or merges with) another and pays more than its accounting value (i.e., what the balance sheet reflects as its value). The difference is called goodwill.</li><li>The buyer is paying for goodwill as though it were an asset.</li><li>Goodwill is a growing aspect of many large organizations' financial value.</li><li>Goodwill (the value of "intangibles") can often become more than 50% of a buyer's financial value.</li><li>Many prevention costs, that are treated as annual expenses when initially incurred, form part of the underlying investments (value) that results in goodwill.</li><li>Goodwill (asset) is checked every year for impairment, and if it is considered impaired the buyer has to write off the amount of the impairment.</li><li>Lack of understanding of the value of an effective culture and the investments incurred to create and maintain it, results in its value being depleted by a buyer.</li><li>A better understanding between culture and financial investments incurred to create and sustain it would provide some additional transparency to the management of goodwill.</li></ul>

Checklist
• Is the organization involved in mergers or acquisitions?
• Is there any tracking of cumulative expenditures involved in creating and sustaining culture?
• Is the management of human capital seen as an investment that creates value?
• Are these notional investments adjusted for aspects such as length of service and turnover?
• Does the organization know the core aspects of its approach to a positive culture? What are the key investments?

13 Integrated reporting

The evolution of integrated reporting was discussed in Chapter 2 and can now be reviewed related to the costs of a poor culture. In many ways, a poor culture is a lack of system integration. The various models that have been developed – the <IR> approach in particular – strive to shift the bias in reporting to a system in which the interests of all key stakeholders are addressed.

It has been argued that business has historically been biased in favor of the stakeholders who provide capital and that the interests of others have had to be more accommodating. The <IR> framework allows for the assessment of materiality among the interests of stakeholders and develops several categories of providers of resources to the organization. A key goal is to encourage integrated thinking where the organization is seen as a "whole system" rather than the sum of its parts.

Historically, the optimum way to assess system performance was through financial results, the assumption being that if financial performance was healthy, management was doing its job. However, it has been demonstrated that successful financial performance is not always a good indicator of the underlying health of a system. Epic failures such as those of Enron and Carillion have demonstrated this. But has the evolution of integrated reporting resulted in a shift to integrated thinking? It seems that is not yet the case. To explore this further, we start with a review of the core resources that <IR> has chosen as the basis for stakeholder reporting – referred to as "capitals":

Capital	Summary inclusion
Financial	The pool of funds that is available to the organization for use in the production of goods or the provision of services obtained through financing, such as debt, equity, or grants, or generated through operations or investments.
Manufactured	Manufactured physical objects (as distinct from natural physical objects) that are available to the organization for use in the production of goods or the provision of services, including: buildings, equipment, and infrastructure (such as roads, ports, bridges and waste and water treatment plants).
Intellectual	Intangibles that provide competitive advantage, including intellectual property, such as patents, copyrights, software and organizational systems, procedures, and protocols; the intangibles that are associated with the brand and reputation that an organization has developed.
Human	People's skills and experience, and their capacity and motivations to innovate, including their: alignment with and support of the organization's governance framework and ethical values such as its recognition of human rights; ability to understand and implement an organization's strategy; loyalties and motivations for improving processes, goods, and services, including their ability to lead and to collaborate
Social and relationship	The institutions and relationships established within and between each community, group of stakeholders and other networks to enhance individual and collective well-being. Social and relationship capital includes common values and behaviours; key relationships, and the trust and loyalty that an organization has developed and strives to build and protect with customers, suppliers, and business partners; an organization's social licence to operate
Natural	Natural capital is an input to the production of goods or the provision of services. An organization's activities also impact, positively or negatively, on natural capital. It includes water, land, minerals, and forests; biodiversity and eco-system health

There are well established structures for financial capital reporting; there are also mandatory compliance requirements in other areas such as health and safety relative to human capital and environmental requirements related to natural capital. What has not yet emerged are two critical components.

1. An alternative to financial performance as a "whole system" indicator of system health.
2. New metrics that depict the health of each of the other capitals relative to the performance of the overall system.

One of the challenges for integrated reporting and one which the cost of poor culture may start to address, is the silo thinking that still permeates many organizations. Accountability and responsibility at the "C-suite" level continue to be organized around functional roles and specializations, and this makes integrated reporting and accountability under the six capitals prone to a silo-based approach.

Capital	Who might be tasked with reporting
Financial	Typically, CFO, whose primary focus is driven by statutory requirements and standards compliance
Manufactured	Operational, part of financial and possibly environmental
Intellectual	Could be HR, legal and/or accounting relative to intellectual property
Human	Typically, HR
Social and relationship	Sales and possibly supply chain management; possibly legal relative to non-operational issues
Natural	Environmental

The result may tend to be an integrated report populated with various functional indicators that center around key performance indicators (KPIs) relative to a particular resource. What will often be missing will be the relationship between resources. As an example, one of the SASB (one of a group of organizations working towards commonality among reporting standards) lists the three main aspects – **General Issue Categories (GIC)** – as employee health and safety, labor practices, and employee diversity, inclusion, and engagement. This shows a clear bias towards compliance and guidance requirements relative to managing HR rather than consideration of the impact of HR as a core component of the system.

The Prince's Accounting for Sustainability Project (A4S), a group of financial managers committed to building the finance role in sustainability reporting, is developing approaches for finance to support integrated reporting, but there is little talk of the impact of culture on system performance. Nor does there appear to be any discussion on the issue of intangibles and the linkages between operating expenditures, i.e., cost and HR performance. Examples and case studies have been produced in an attempt to create a value of the workforce, but this adds little to an understanding of the connection between system performance and workforce engagement – i.e., a positive culture.

In its proposals for HR metrics, SASB links its responses, and comments on examples of how other organizations are reporting by the qualifier that there *"are certain areas that investors do not seem to have an interest in."* Maybe the danger in this approach is that, while investors feel that they understand the organizational risks and are happy with annual returns, there will be little effort to ask why corporate reporting is unable to alert shareholders to problems, such as at Carillion, that are clearly related to the organization's culture?

In *How Accountants Lost their Balance* (Shepherd 2021), the author attempts to alert the profession to the underlying shifts that have been taking place in the economy, changing the way financial resources are being deployed. Not only are the negative costs of poor culture hidden in operating expenses, but significant amounts of funding are also being applied to fund intangibles as a critical component of many organizations' operational capability.

Current financial reporting discloses neither of these, yet both pose risks to the investor. Much of the funding of intangibles is being applied to prevention costs in the COPC model, yet this is invisible. What is worse, for the investor, these costs are included in annual operating expenses, yet their goal is to create long-term value for the organization through the workforce; there is no visibility into whether the organizational culture is generating the maximum ROI from these investments.

This is where the linkages of failure costs become so important in building a bridge between financial reporting and human capital. If turnover numbers are higher, then the organization is losing the benefit of these investments faster than its competitors, ultimately increasing the cost of doing business. The same would be true of "social and relationship" capital if organizational culture were not building loyalty to the brand and enhancing organizational reputation.

One might be tempted to conclude that many investors "don't know what they don't know" and, in the same way that a poor culture poses the risk of financial surprises internally, so it poses a risk to investors. Every dollar of excess cost caused by poor culture is coming from investor value and wealth creation; every penalty paid or fine awarded comes from the investors.

Integrated reporting, to be successful, needs to build bridges between functions so that all stakeholders understand the risk resulting from the way in which the business is being run as well as the risk to the system as a whole.

Integrated reporting, summary
• An effective culture is *de facto* a sign of systemic thinking around an integrated organization.
• Human capital reporting is one of six key aspects of integrated reporting under the <IR> framework.
• Human capital is part of a system of resources that is integrated within a business model.
• As one of six capitals, integrated reporting of human capital should reflect the health and contribution of that aspect of the overall system.
• All capitals are inter-dependent e.g., human capital consumes financial capital but creates social, relationship and intellectual capital.
• Effective integrated reporting should demonstrate the relationships and dependencies between the capitals.
• Developing a "cost of culture" approach can be a positive step in developing these depictions of inter-dependency.
• Opportunity exists to develop HR metrics to reflect systemic contribution and not just HR activity and compliance.
Checklist
• Is the organization interested / involved in integrated reporting?
• Has the approach shifted to a cross-functional enterprise approach, or is it currently focused on metrics created mainly by functional areas of accountability?
• Is there a growing understanding of how human capital contributes to success of the system in terms of overall performance?

14 Behavior-based cost control

For financial managers, cost control is a key focus. Management accountants within an organization are constantly expected to provide line managers with an understanding of cost behavior and identify where opportunity for improvement exists. Finance is often expected to be the champion of cost control. Payroll cost is one of largest expenses and consumers of cash flow and as such provides an ideal target for cost reduction. Yet few financial managers know where the money is going. They know who is spending it but not why. If there is no understanding between the funding going to intangibles and their importance and impact of future business activity, arbitrary reductions to payroll costs can destroy "intangible capability."

Tools such as ABC or Activity Based Costing have been applied by organizations to understanding the drivers of expenditure. Yet in discussion with a leading North American specialist in ABC, who has been involved in many implementations, his opinion was that few organizations have any idea of how much cash is being directed to building or sustaining intangibles.

One key aspect of an effective culture is a commitment to continual improvement; this concept is at the heart of cultures such as at Toyota. Most of this book has focused on understanding and developing an approach for the identification of excess costs and lost opportunities relative to a poor culture. For financial managers, this linkage between culture and cost goes far beyond effective people-centric strategies and focuses on the ability to control costs at every level, by every person within the organization.

While the goals of reducing cost have remained constant, the areas of focus for achieving this have shifted from direct costs to indirect ones, particularly labor costs. In manufacturing organizations, direct materials and direct labor have been well understood for a long time. Continual efforts to drive down direct labor costs through automation, simplification, the elimination of tasks, and other process improvements have delivered considerable benefits. When the only opportunity left to reduce labor costs, is to reduce the hourly rate, the solution has been to outsource to lower-cost environments.

Indirect costs in many organizations have typically been controlled by responsibility centers — attributing costs to cost centers controlled by managers and tracking costs by expense type. Reductions were typically achieved by a constant focus on headcount reductions and the stringent control of expenses.

As direct costs are driven down and/or outsourced, a larger portion of costs becomes the result of supplier negotiations; direct labor plus direct material is now combined as a negotiated supplier cost; as a result, effective relationships with suppliers focusing on mutual efforts to reduce cost become more critical. Culture plays a key part in building this collaboration and creating an effective "system."

As direct costs have been driven down, indirect costs become a larger portion of the cost base. Efforts to reduce costs through headcount reductions often produce dysfunctional outcomes, as individual managers drive their own costs down while creating negative impacts elsewhere within an organization. This impact of silo-based management has been recognized as causing problems since many internal process's cross organizational boundaries, i.e., silos.

Operational process activities are highly interdependent, and cost reductions in one area create operational problems and cost pressures for other areas. In order to address this challenge, managers must be able to collaborate and cooperate for the mutual benefit of the whole organization rather than focusing on individual results. Once again, culture - especially effective trust and communications are key enablers. Individual based goals and compensation tend to constrain this potential.

Finally, in any area of work that touches the client or customer, efforts to reduce across-the-board headcount cuts generally result in declining operational capability, client service, and reputation. This can be seen in marketing, sales, engineering and design, accounting, human resources, information technology, and other areas. It decreases the capability of an organization – and thus the intangible (goodwill) value. A culture that seeks a "whole system" approach with the people plus the customer at the center provide a key building block to address these challenges.

As the architecture of an organization's activity changes, the approaches to planning, controlling, managing, reporting, and reducing costs must also change. An approach to behavior-based cost management was proposed by the author[28], which suggests a framework that has organizational culture at its center. The approach focuses on the belief that lack of employee engagement will lead to cost control challenges. These will often have been met by periodic programs of focused cost reduction, where incentives will be offered for ideas and suggestions to cut costs. These of often result in headcount reductions rather than re-deploying staff, which usually worsens the culture situation. That article was followed up by an in-depth management accounting guideline[29] in 2016.

---

[28] *Strategic Finance magazine* (IMA), July/August 2015. "Human aspects of cost management," (by Nick A. Shepherd).

[29] Shepherd, Nick A., April 2016. *The Behavioral Aspects of Cost Management.* Statements in Management Accounting, Institute of Management Accountants.

This approach to behavior-based cost management – the "5C model" – is made up of five aspects with **organizational culture** as the primary or core aspect:

Business Planning Framework	Cost Elements	Explanation of Financial Aspects
Purpose	Culture	The foundational approach to planning and running the enterprise—a combination of task (mission) and relationship values that guide behavior
Passion	Caring	Building the culture—engaging the resources required to convert intent to action in a way that reflects care about cost minimization
Process	Communication	Alignment of business process and resource allocation to execution of task and clarity of communication of costs aspects and impacts to decision makers
People	Collaboration	Aligning values with human engagement, often through processes and partnerships, by converting "intent" into action through effective collaboration and coordination
Performance	Continuity	Approaches to sustaining cost improvement as a core strategy through continual improvement and cost "life cycle" thinking

While a commitment to culture as a key strategy is the foundation, the next four aspects refer to deployment. More information on how to develop and apply a framework for managing corporate culture is contained in the author's book *Corporate Culture* (see Bibliography). Each of the five segments in the business model demonstrate how accounting works to ensure that the linkage between culture and accountability for cost management and control are addressed. In the **Culture** section, there are several areas for finance involvement:

Aspect	Finance Responsibility	Finance Influence
Ensuring concept of value and intangibles is understood	√	√
Communicating with and ensuring that owners/shareholders understand risk related of intangibles and impact on sustainability		√
Ensuring a clear, sustained statement of mission and values		√
Ensuring that goals and KPIs include task (outcomes) and relationship (behaviors)	√	√
Ensuring alignment of policies and procedures with stated values	√	√
Ensuring investment in leadership development of all managers	√	√
Avoiding short-term financial guidance	√	√

For finance / accounting an important function will be to help persuade other functional leaders, as well as the CEO and members of the board, that a considerable amount of organizational value is tied up with items that are not included in the financial records – the intangibles. While these are not reflected in the records, significant resources are applied to funding their development as part of ongoing operational expenses; however, their reporting and visibility is at a high level and understanding is usually limited. The COPC assessment assists in extracting some of these costs and can support efforts to demonstrate the strategic importance. A key aspect for accounting will be to understand the importance of digging into the numbers and asking, "what exactly are we paying people to do?"

The next phase is to develop an attitude of **Caring** about cost – some may even call this an aspect of responsible stewardship. Waste of *any* resources be it money, natural, or human resources, is unethical. Accounting cannot control costs, as most decisions that impact the consumption of resources, which in turn must be funded and thus consume financial resources, are made by operational line managers and other employees across an organization.

Each of the areas shown below will be important in developing an attitude of caring about the use of limited resources; one aspect discussed earlier is the excess cost of control systems that are sometimes a cost of poor culture, particularly where leaders feel that the only way to control risk is to limit delegations of authority. The problem is that people still have to get the job done and, as a result, they find ways around the controls.

Aspect	Finance Responsibility	Finance Influence
Aligned, trained, and effective leadership at all levels	√	√
Culture of engagement in planning	√	√
Inclusive organizational structure—limited hierarchy		√
Control systems that enable the work of the business	√	
Effective compensation, and reward and recognition systems		√
Operating procedure alignment		√
Performance rewards that address tasks and relationships		√

Finance must take the lead in evaluating corporate risk and controls to ensure that the organization is "just in control." Excessive controls can inhibit the innovation and creativity needed to stimulate ideas that improve operational effectiveness. Excessive costs are often incurred – and sometimes go unnoticed – when front-line staff develop ways of getting around excessive controls. Maintenance staff are often unfairly accused of hiding spare parts and inventories, but they feel compelled to do so due to requisitioning and purchasing policies that slow down the purchase of parts needed for repair of equipment, and thus negatively impact capacity utilization and equipment uptime.

Ultimately, ineffective purchasing policies drive up the overall cost of business by encouraging actions such as just-in-case (JIC) inventory management – another excess cost of poor culture. In addition, the search for the lowest bidder often drives up administration costs that eat away at unit cost savings through higher process costs in areas such as purchasing, receiving, inventory management, and payables.

Duplication of generic interchangeable parts can also occur when inventories are managed by vendor part number and when the Purchasing department constantly changes vendors, resulting in higher inventory and often unplanned obsolescence. This would again be a cost of poor culture related to the lack of trusting, collaborative relationships with suppliers.

To enable a culture for cost, the elimination of waste, and continual improvement, accounting / finance must reflect on the manner in which financial information is **Communicated** to others in the organization. These aspects are shown below:

Aspect	Finance Responsibility	Finance Influence
Cost architecture aligned with business	√	
Clear cost drivers/process links and alignment	√	
Clear responsibility/accountability and no allocations	√	
Reports available on demand and in operational language	√	√
Training—finance for nonfinancial managers	√	√

In many situations, there is a lack of alignment between what is being managed and how costs are presented. People are compensated to perform tasks: where these tasks occur as part of a planned process, there may be opportunities to improve the process and so reduce the resources consumed. This would be the focus of continual improvement. However, people also respond to events that may not be planned and thus spend time on tasks that might otherwise be avoided. Such events would form a portion of the events identified during the COPC action plan outlined in Chapter 10.

Finance will also play a key role in the cultural change, in which drivers of unnecessary costs relate to relationships.

Often, because cost information is provided on a silo-based responsibility basis, there is little visibility of the excess costs that occur due to poor collaboration between departments – where the actions of one area to reduce costs can impact work and increase costs down the line. Process cost visibility would help demonstrate this and create a base for process cost improvement for the benefit of the system. Providing the information in a way that aligns with decision making might include the following:

Aspect	Finance Responsibility	Finance Influence
Provision of process-based cost information	√	
Development of cross-functional teams/process teams		√
Benefit sharing across departments	√	√
Benefit sharing with suppliers and subcontractors		√
Benefit sharing with distributors and clients		√

To enable cross-functional **Collaboration** to work, even when the correct accounting information is provided, will require the development of skills, for which funding must be made available. Excess costs are often driven by poor relationships between an organization and its external stakeholders, such as suppliers and clients. To enhance system performance, the culture must move to a win/win scenario rather than a win/lose one, so that both parties have an incentive to reduce overall costs and share the benefits. This is a paradigm shift, especially for financial management and supplier management. Finance can help build the business case to ensure that where *real* savings are created there is an ability to share benefits.

The final stage in the culture- or behavior-based approach to cost management is to embed the behavioral aspects into the culture – "the way we do business." This provides a foundation for **Continuity**. Many initiatives, especially around cost reduction, fail because they are seen as "programs" that have a start and end. Accounting must embrace the new way of thinking on a permanent basis; one of the key dangers is that cost reduction becomes an issue when times are bad but is considered to be less serious when times are good. Cost reduction is *always* an issue.

Aspect	Finance Responsibility	Finance Influence
Understand and reinforce life-cycle thinking	√	√
Avoid cost reduction initiatives as only "programs"	√	√
Constantly communicate "business reality"		√
Identify, track, and communicate and share savings	√	

A lot of behavior is based on perception and two key areas in the above chart are worthy of reinforcement. First, good, regular, and honest communication with all employees about organizational performance is an essential element of building trust and commitment; second, it is always important for people to have a context within which to compare their own organization to others.

Regular updates to employees about comparable market and organizational information will help keep them grounded, and more willing to recognize the ongoing competitive pressures as well as the need for vigilance in both cost minimization and other key strategic changes. (Replace Rah Rah with Reality?)

In summary, the 5C model is reflected in the image below. Culture is at the heart, while effective approaches identified as caring, communications, collaboration, and continuation would provide the underlying financial conduct that supports and complements effective cost control.

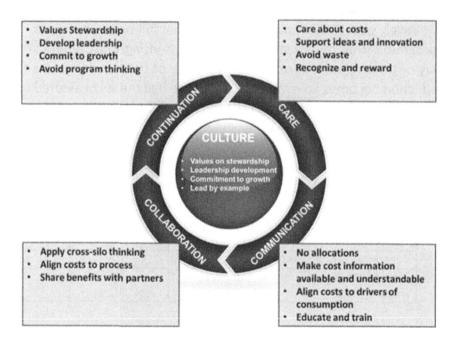

The core aspects of a cost control culture are reinforced in the center and are foundations of any behavior-based approach:

- Values that embed collective responsible stewardship
- Leadership development – leaders who support a culture of responsible stewardship.
- A commitment to growth (and not success by shrinking)
- Leadership by example – leaders who demonstrate they care about cost control.

While an effective culture is the foundation of cost management, it also creates a permanent basis of an organization's ability to be "change ready" (as has already been discussed). This readiness underpins innovation, creativity, and responsiveness to both reduce cycle time and increase the speed of response to change.

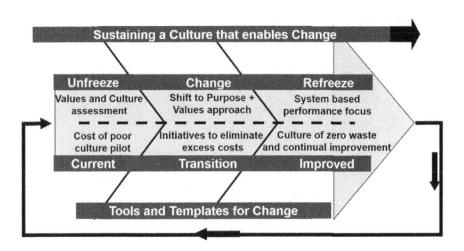

As an organization makes a strategic shift to become more balanced between elements of the system and to optimize system performance and organizational sustainability, the accounting / finance / cost management function must be part of the change. Hidden costs buried in operating expenses must be extracted and shown as being areas for improvement.

In the "Unfreeze" phase, as the organization shifts its thinking to understand its culture through an assessment, and start the values development and deployment process, the financial area will be a partner by developing a pilot approach to understanding the costs of poor culture. In the "Change" phase, where values and purpose (behavior and task) become equally important in strategy, the reporting of the costs of poor culture will further develop and be seen as an opportunity to change behavioral aspects of the business to improve performance. Finally in the third phase, as the organization seeks to embed its new way of doing business, performance will be judged on system sustainability, together with short-term performance, to seek system optimization. The supporting financial information will be aligned to enable opportunities for improvement anywhere within or outside the organization, with its key stakeholders, to be understood and demonstrated. As business strategy changes, so will the approach of individual functions such as Finance and Accounting need to shift.

Behavior-based cost control, summary
• Costs are controlled by people not accounting.
• Cost control is a function of human engagement and the elimination of waste.
• Effective cost continual is founded on a culture of continual improvement (in all things).
• Organizational culture is at the heart of an effective approach to cost management.
• Behavioral based costing shifts the focus and ownership of cost management to those using (all) the resources.
• The behavior-based cost model is aligned with a 5P business model: Purpose, Passion, Process, People, and Performance.
• The behavior-based cost model is a 5C framework of: Culture, Caring, Communication, Collaboration, and Continuity.
• Behavior-based costing aligns with, and is built on, an effective organizational culture.
• The development of a cost of culture model for understanding resource consumption is consistent with behavior-based costing.
• Finance plays a key role in aligning corporate culture with effective cost management.
• Finance has full responsibility for some aspects and is an influencer in areas where others have accountability.
• Cultural development and implementing cost of culture are complementary activities.

Checklist
• Are organizational costs being continually reduced by employee ideas and suggestions?
• Is accountability for cost seen as an accounting issue or as a shared enterprise challenge (i.e., systemic)?
• Do employees have full visibility into cost information and targets for resource consumption within their control?
• Are costs seen as a process-driven issue or as a functional / departmental issue?
• Is the approach to HR management conducive to cost reduction and improvement (i.e., redeployment, retraining or other approaches to reassign staff)?
• Do leaders at all levels demonstrate responsible stewardship through prudent expenditures and a focus on waste of any sort?

Bibliography

Becker, Brian. E., Huselid, Mark. A., and Ulrich, F. Dave (2001) *The HR scorecard,* Harvard Business Press.

Blanchard, Ken, and O'Connor, Michael (1997) *Managing by Values*, Berrett-Koehler.

Campanella, Jack (1999) *Principles of Quality Costs, 3rd edition*, Quality Press, ASQ.

Cohen, Ben, and Warwick, Mal (2006) *Values Driven Business*, Berrett-Koehler.

Crosby, Phil (1979) *Quality is Free*, Signet.

Edvinsson, L., and Malone. M. S. (1997) *Intellectual Capital*, pp.168–169, Harper Business.

Fitz-enz, Jac (2000) *The ROI of Human Capital*, AMACOM.

Gleeson-White, Jane (2014) *Six Capitals: The Revolution Capitalism has to have – or can accountants save the planet*, Allen & Unwin.

Hood, Daniel (2019) *Trust is just the beginning*, Accounting Today (Study from ACCA, IFAC, and CA ANZ), March 4.

IFAC (2015) *Materiality in Integrated Reporting*, Integrated Reporting <IR> and International Federation of Accountants.

IIRC (2013) *The International <IR> Framework*, International Integrated Reporting Council, December.

Lev, Baruch, and Gu, Feng (2016) *The End of Accounting*, Wiley.

Johnson, Thomas. H., and Kaplan, Robert, S. (1987) *Relevance Lost: The Rise and Fall of Management Accounting*, Harvard Business School Press.

Kaplan, Robert. S., and Norton, David. P. (1996) *The Balanced Scorecard*, Harvard Business Review Press.

Kaplan, Robert. S., and Norton, David. P. (2006) *Alignment*, Harvard Business School Publishing.

Kearns. P., and Woollard, Stuart (2019) *The Mature Corporation*, Cambridge Scholars Press.

Liker, Jeffrey. K. (2011) *Toyota Under Fire: How Toyota faced the challenges of the recall and came out stronger*, McGraw Hill.

Liker, Jeffrey. K. (2004) *The Toyota Way*, McGraw Hill.

Liker, Jeffrey. K., and Hoseus, Michael (2008) *Toyota Culture: The Heart and Soul of the Toyota Way*, McGraw Hill.

Liker, Jeffrey. K., and Meier, David. P. (2007) *Toyota Talent; Developing Your People the Toyota Way*, McGraw Hill.

Magee, David (2007) *How Toyota Became #1*, Portfolio.

Nayar, Vineet (2010) *Employees First, Customers Second*, Harvard Business Press.

Peters, Sandra (2020) *FASB Turns Up the Heat on Goodwill Impairment Testing*, CFA Institute, February 12.

Rother, Mike (2010) *Toyota Kata*, McGraw Hill.

Schmidt, Eric., and Rosenberg, Jonathan (2014) *How Google Works*, Hachette Book Group Ltd.

Shepherd, N. (2005) *Governance, Accountability and Sustainable Development: An agenda for the 21st century*, Thomson Carswell, Canada.

Shepherd, N., and Adams, M. (2014) *Unrecognized Intangible Assets: Identification, Management and Reporting*, Statements in Management Accounting series, Institute of Management Accountants.

Shepherd, N. (2021) *How Accountants Lost their Balance*, Kindle Direct Publishing (Eduvision / Jannas Publications).

Shepherd, N. (2021) *Corporate Culture – Combining Purpose and Values*, Kindle Direct Publishing (Eduvision / Jannas Publications).

Smyth, Peter, and Shepherd. N. (2012) *Reflective Leaders and High-Performance Organizations*, iUniverse Publishing.

Stewart, T. (1997) *Intellectual Capital: The New Wealth of organizations*, pp. 232–233, Doubleday.

Stewart, Tom (1997) *Intellectual Capital: The New Wealth of Nations*, Currency Doubleday.

Wallis, Jim (2010) *Rediscovering Values*, Simon & Schuster.

Weiss, David. S. (2000) *High Performance HR – Leveraging Human Resources for Competitive Advantage*, John Wiley.

The Cost of Poor Culture

NICK A. SHEPHERD
FCPA, FCGA, FCCA, FCMC

Nick has over 50 years of varied work experience including senior general management and finance roles. From 1989 to 2017 he ran his own management consulting and professional development company. Currently he is officially retired but still spends time on research and writing, focusing his efforts in the areas of organizational sustainability, human capital, and integrated reporting. Nick has experience working in and with private family business, public corporations, governments, and NPOs. Nick is currently a Director and Council member of the UK-based Maturity Institute.

As a management consultant and facilitator, Nick designed and presented many professional development workshops, internationally and across Canada. Nick was also part-time faculty member at Grenoble Graduate School of Business (GGSB), where he taught modules on Mergers and Acquisitions, and Management Consulting; he also lectured at McMaster / DeGroote on ethics; and led the Professional Standards Committee of the International Council of Management Consultants in developing the competency model that now forms the basis of CMC certification in over 50 global CMC Institutes. In 2007, Nick received the President's Award for Education from the Certified General Accountants of British Columbia. Nick's consulting work has included both public- and private-sector clients in many countries, including Canada, the USA, the UK, the Caribbean, South Africa, Kazakhstan, Kyrgyzstan, Uzbekistan, and Jordan.

Nick joined CPA Ontario as a Fellow in 2014 following the merger of accounting bodies. Prior to that Nick was a CGA for over 35 years, obtaining his Fellowship in 2009. Nick is a Fellow of the Chartered Association of Certified Accountants (FCCA UK), and a Fellow of the Institute of Certified Management Consultants of Ontario (FCMC – Honor Roll), and Past President of the Institute. Nick is also Past Chair of the National Certification Committee for all Institutes of Management Consulting across Canada, and Past Chair of the Professional Standards Committee of the International Council of Management Consulting Institutes (ICMCI). He served as one of four trustees for Canada at the International level (ICMCI). Nick has also been a member of Mensa for many years.

Nick has authored several books, including *How Accountants Lost their Balance* (2021), *Corporate Culture* (2021), *Governance, Accountability and Sustainable Development* (2005), *Controllers Handbook* (2003, second edition 2008), and *Variance Analysis* (1980); he co-authored, with Dr. Peter Smyth, *Reflective Leaders and High-Performing Organizations* (2012). Among several other books and articles that Nick has authored are: *Values and Ethics: From Inception to Practice*, *The Evolution of Accountability – Sustainability Reporting for Accountants*, *Unrecognized Intangible Assets: Identification, Management and Reporting*, and *The Human Aspects of Cost Control*. Nick also developed several Ethics courses for accountants and consultants, both nationally and internationally.

Contact Nick at nick@eduvision.ca